FOR YOUR INFORMATION 2

INTERMEDIATE READING SKILLS

Karen Blanchard ◆ Christine Root

Longman

For Your Information 2

Addison-Wesley Longman, 10 Bank Street, White Plains, NY 10606

Editorial Director: Joanne Dresner
Acquisitions Editor: Allen Ascher
Development Editor: Françoise Leffler
Production Editor: Lisa Hutchins
Photo Research: Brian Huss
Text Design: Taurins Design Associates
Cover Design: Taurins Design Associates

Text Art: Yoshi Miyake 10, 75, 83, 107, 109, 160; Michael Moran 11, 12, 13, 16, 125, 126, 148, 150, 170, 172, 178, 182, 184, 186, 196.

Grateful acknowledgment is given to the following for providing photographs or text art: p.4, Liaison International © Charles Nes; p.32, Reuters/Bettmann; p.36, The Image Bank © Walter Looss; p.42, Gamma-Liaison © Morimoto; p.45, Woodbury & Associates © 1991 Jon van Woerden; p.50, International Stock Photo © Ryan Williams; p.64, International Stock Photo © Johnny Stockshooter; p.69, UPI/Bettmann; p.94, Photo by Linda Wyman; p. 101, The Image Bank © Harald Sund; p. 120, Levi Strauss & Company; p. 136, © 1993 Robert Lorenz; p. 155, UPI/Bettmann; p. 171, Ali M. Bayraktaroglu; p. 179, Debra Wilson; p. 187, The Image Bank © David W. Hamilton; p.200, Stock Boston © Mike Mazzaschi; p.203, Patrick Alias; p.204, Alison G. Howe; p.206, Thidarat Siriphativirat

Text credits appear on page 216.

Library of Congress Cataloging-in-Publication Data
Blanchard, Karen Lourie, 1951-
    For your information 2 / Karen Blanchard, Christine Root.
      p. cm.
    ISBN 0-201-82538-4
    1. English language—Textbooks for foreign speakers. 2. Readers.
I. Root, Christine Baker, 1945- . II. Title.
PE1128.B586 1995
428.6'4—dc20   95-24397
                                 CIP

8 9 10-CRS-00 99 98

This book is dedicated to our sons
Daniel, Ian, and Matthew,
whose curiosity about the world
keeps them, and us, reading.

CONTENTS

For Your Information 2 is a book of authentic readings for intermediate students of English as a Second Language. It is a reading skill-builder designed for use in ESL adult education programs, universities, language institutes, and secondary schools both in the United States and abroad.

For Your Information 2 is made up of eight thematically based units, each of which contains a selection of three or four articles, stories, essays, and interviews. It is based on research that indicates that ESL students are able to read at a higher level of English than they can produce. Relevant skill-building activities, both written and oral, accompany each unit as a whole and each individual reading.

The book is designed to help students become comfortable, competent, independent readers. It engages them in the process of reading thoughtfully, and it encourages them to move beyond passive reading to a more active, sophisticated analysis of the material. To this end, students are asked to integrate and understand new ideas as well as use their own general knowledge and experience for follow-up activities. Although it is a reading text, students practice their speaking, listening, writing, and analytical skills throughout *For Your Information 2*. The tasks are varied, accessible, and engaging and provide stimuli for frequent interaction.

The readings are controlled in the sense that the language is relatively simple and straightforward; the readings do, however, become increasingly difficult as one progresses through the text.

The basic format for each unit in *For Your Information 2* is as follows:

● **Points to Ponder**
These prereading questions introduce the topic of the unit and get students thinking about the topic.

● **Reading Selections and Skill-Building Tasks**
Each unit contains from three to four authentic reading selections on topics of high interest and universal appeal and concern. Selections are accompanied by a combination of comprehension questions and activities to practice skimming, scanning, finding main and supporting ideas, separating fact from opinion, predicting, outlining, determining meaning of vocabulary from context, or using correct word forms.

● **Tying It All Together**
Coming at the end of each unit, this section provides
—a word game, "Just for Fun," made up of words from the unit
—questions that encourage students to think about and discuss the
ideas they have read about in the unit
—a Reader's Journal, for students to reflect in writing on the readings of the unit

We hope that you and your students enjoy working together on the
readings in this text and that you enjoy and find them interesting
for your information, too.

KLB, CBR

ACKNOWLEDGMENTS

We would like to thank first and foremost our families for their unending patience and interest in this project. They deserve special mention for giving so freely of their time and creative energy.

Our thanks go also to our friends, colleagues, and students for agreeing to read just one more article and try out just one more activity. To Hasan Halkali, Lynn Meng, and Christian and Molly Sherden, thank you for your insightful suggestions.

Last, but most definitely not least, we want to thank Allen Ascher and Joanne Dresner at Addison-Wesley Longman for their faith in us.

CROSS-CULTURAL CONNECTIONS

Selections

A custom is a practice followed by people from a particular culture. It is their usual way of doing something. Customs, like language, vary from one culture to another.

This unit contains several articles about the different ways people behave around the world. Sometimes these differences are interesting, but they can also cause confusion or even embarrassment.

Think about and then discuss the following questions.

1. In the United States, people shake hands when they meet someone new. Americans might kiss each other if they are relatives or old friends. Other American customs include giving presents on birthdays, eating turkey on Thanksgiving, lighting fireworks on the Fourth of July, and singing the national anthem before baseball games. Think about some of the customs in your culture and answer the following questions.

    a. What do you do when you meet someone new?

    _____

    _____

    b. How do you celebrate birthdays?

    _____

    _____

    c. What do you do when your favorite sports team wins?

    _____

    _____

2. Why do you think knowledge of cultures and gestures is important in communication? List some specific reasons to support your idea.

    _____

    _____

Kissing Your Way around the World is an article written from the point of view of a citizen of the United States. The author discusses the different meanings kissing has around the world.

BEFORE YOU READ

PREREADING ACTIVITY

Think about when and why people kiss in your culture. Make a list of those times and share it with your classmates.

_____

_____

_____

_____

FIRST READING

As you read the article, try to discover how many different meanings a kiss can have.

● ●

Kissing Your Way around the World

L E S L I E   D E N D Y

1   What in the world is kissing good for? That depends on where in the world you are (or were).

2   A kiss means "I love you" in many countries—but not everywhere. European explorers found plenty of places where people had never even heard of kissing. The Ainu people of Japan liked to *bite* their lovers' cheeks. Eskimos rubbed their noses together instead, and so did certain African tribes and Pacific islanders.

3   In other places people would just put their noses close to their lovers' faces and sniff. Many Malay tribes did this, and probably the ancient Egyptians. In several languages the word for "kiss" means "smell."

4   Kisses are also good for saying hello. Do you kiss relatives on the cheek when you visit them? If you live in Europe or South America, you see many more of these greeting kisses. Some men kiss each other on the cheeks at business meetings. It's like shaking hands.

5   Traveling from one country to another can get confusing if you don't know the rules for greeting one another. Many European men and women say hello with two kisses, one on each cheek. But three kisses are polite in Belgium, and young people in Paris often prefer four. You *must* start with the right cheek. Starting with the left would be as awkward as sticking out your left hand for a handshake.

6   A variation on the cheek kiss is found in Brazil. When ladies meet, they put their cheeks together and kiss the air.

7   Kissing was even more common in ancient times. The Hebrews, Christians, Greeks, and Romans kissed a lot—family, friends, and perfect strangers. The Romans might have kissed anyone they met on the hand, the cheek, or the mouth. They often put a perfume such as myrrh in their mouths to make the kisses more pleasant.

8   Another thing kisses were good for in olden times was for sealing a promise. For over five hundred years, the knights in Europe knelt down before their lords in special homage ceremonies. The knight promised to fight for the lord, and the lord promised to give the knight a piece of land near the castle. Then the men kissed each other on the mouth. This ceremony lasted until the 1500s.

9   Have you ever seen a row of XXXXXs at the bottom of a letter, meaning kisses? That comes from the time of knights and castles, too. The X started out as a type of signature. In the Middle Ages many people could not write their names. A person would sign an X on a paper (symbolizing a cross), and then kiss it to promise that he would stick to the deal. Now an X just means a kiss.

10   Kisses can also show respect. People kiss religious statues and flags. They have kissed the feet and footprints of kings and queens, as well as their hands, knees, and robes. Roman students kissed their teachers' hands. Sometimes people kiss the ground when they come home to a country they love.

11   Europeans and Latin Americans say "beautiful!" by kissing their fingertips when they see a pretty girl, a Ferrari, or a great soccer play. But you can also say "good-bye" to someone by kissing your fingertips and blowing the kiss away.

12   Did you ever kiss a hurt finger to make it well? That custom comes from England. People used to think kisses had magic powers. The French started kissing their cards for good luck in gambling, and some people still kiss a pair of dice before they roll them. And don't forget all the magical kisses in fairy tales that were supposed to waken the sleeping princess or turn a beast into a prince.

13   Humans may be the only animals who believe in magic, but we're not the only animals who kiss. Chimpanzees greet each other with little pecks or big, widemouthed kisses. They also kiss to make up after a fight. When prairie dogs meet, they kiss each other to see who's a family member and who's a stranger. Fish called "kissing gouramis" press their mouths together like suction cups.

14   Kissing will probably still be around a thousand years from now, but the rules may keep changing. Even a piece of mistletoe[1] on the ceiling can change the rules for a few days.

The world's longest kiss on record lasted 17 days and $10\frac{1}{2}$ hours.

---

[1]mistletoe A plant with small white berries. At Christmastime, small branches of the plant are hung over doorways in people's homes for decoration. According to tradition, if someone stands under the mistletoe, it means that this person wants to be kissed.

● ●

HOW WELL DID YOU READ?

Read the following statements. If a statement is true, write _T_ on the line. If it is false, write _F_.

_____ 1. A kiss means the same thing all over the world.

_____ 2. In many places a kiss is a kind of greeting.

_____ 3. Kissing is more popular now than ever before.

_____ 4. In ancient times, a kiss was used to seal a promise.

_____ 5. Kisses can be a sign of respect.

_____ 6. Humans are the only animals that kiss.

IDENTIFYING THE MAIN IDEA

A reading passage often has one main idea. This idea is present throughout the whole passage and represents the general message of the reading.

Which sentence best describes the main idea of the article you have just read? Circle the number of your choice.

1. In many countries a kiss means, "I love you."

2. Kissing is a common form of greeting.

3. Kissing has different meanings in different cultures.

4. Kissing is a sign of respect.

SECOND READING

Now read the article again more carefully. This time, while you read, think about the ways the author supports her ideas.

FINDING SUPPORT FOR MAIN IDEAS

Authors often support their ideas with examples. Find examples in the article to support the following ideas.

1. A kiss is not the only way to express "I love you."

   _____

   _____

2. The rules for kissing depend on what part of the world you are in.

   _____

   _____

3. Kisses can be a sign of respect.

   _____

   _____

4. Humans are not the only animals that kiss.

   _____

   _____

LOCATING INFORMATION

Where do some of the meanings of kissing come from? Look in the article for the history of the following kissing customs.

1. Sealing a promise _____

2. An *X* means a kiss _____

3. Kissing a finger to make it well _____

4. Kissing for good luck _____

FIGURE IT OUT

VOCABULARY IN CONTEXT

It is not always necessary to know the exact meaning of every unfamiliar word you come across. Oftentimes an approximate definition or a general idea of the word is enough to understand the meaning of a sentence or paragraph. You do not need to waste a lot of time looking up every new word in the dictionary. It is important to be able to determine when an exact definition is necessary and when a general meaning is enough.

The Vocabulary in Context exercises in this book will help you develop strategies for understanding new words. The exercises will guide you in using clues such as structure, punctuation, grammar, and the general sense of the sentence. With this information, you should be able to make logical guesses about the meaning of unfamiliar words.

Without using your dictionary, write an approximate definition or a synonym for the highlighted words in the following sentences.

Example 1

When the little boy saw a big spider walking toward him, he became frightened and **dashed** *out of the room.*
(CLUE: What do you think a frightened little boy would do if he saw a big spider?)

  ran _____

Example 2

Unlike his **garrulous** *wife, Jonathan was a man of few words.*
(CLUE: The word *unlike* signals a contrast between Jonathan and his wife. Since you know from the rest of the sentence that Jonathan is "a man of few words," his wife must be a woman of many words.)

  talkative _____

(continued on the next page)

7

1. *In other places people would just put their noses close to their lovers' faces and **sniff**. . . . In several languages the word for "kiss" means "smell."*
(CLUE: What do you do with your nose? What does *kiss* mean in some languages?)

   _____

2. *Kisses are also good for saying hello. Do you kiss relatives on the cheek when you visit them? If you lived in Europe or South America, you would see many more of these **greeting** kisses.*
(CLUE: The word *these* signals that "greeting kisses" have been explained earlier in the text.)

   _____

3. *You must start with the right cheek. Starting with your left would be as **awkward** as sticking out your left hand for a handshake.*
(CLUE: The structure *as . . . as* is used for comparison. In this case, cheek kissing and hand shaking are being compared. Since you normally put out your right hand to shake, starting with your left hand would be *awkward*.)

   _____

4. *A **variation** on the cheek kiss is found in Brazil. When ladies meet, they put their cheeks together and kiss the air.*
(CLUE: Refer to the previous paragraph to find out more information about cheek kisses. You will see that styles of cheek kissing change from one country to another. This should help you guess the meaning of *variation*.)

   _____

5. *They often put a perfume such as **myrrh** in their mouths to make the kisses more pleasant.*
(CLUE: *Such as, for example,* and *for instance* are expressions that introduce an example.)

   _____

6. *The X started out as a type of **signature**. In the Middle Ages many people could not write their names.*
(CLUE: Sometimes the meaning of a word is explained in the next sentence.)

   _____

APPLICATION OF INFORMATION

A. From the article, you learned that the custom of kissing has many meanings. Interview friends, classmates, and teachers to find out about the different meanings of the following customs in different countries. Try to get an example of when to use each one.

1. shaking hands

2. hugging

3. bowing

4. patting someone's back

5. holding hands

6. kissing someone's hand

7. curtseying

B. What other customs can you add to the list from your own culture? Make a list and share it with your classmates.

PROVERBS

A proverb is a short, well-known saying. Read the following proverbs and answer the questions about them. Then discuss your answers with your classmates.

1. There is an old Italian proverb that says, "A kiss on the lips does not always touch the heart." What do you think this proverb means?

_____

_____

2. Another old saying about kissing was written in the 1800s by George Meredith. "Kissing doesn't last, cookery does." Do you agree with this one? Why or why not?

_____

_____

3. Can you think of any proverbs about kissing in your native language?

_____

_____

Gestures are movements of the hands or face that are used to give nonverbal messages. Researchers estimate that the human hands and face can make hundreds of thousands of different signs and expressions. Is it any surprise that gestures and the meanings of the gestures can vary from culture to culture? Understanding the meanings of gestures and being able to use them correctly are important parts of communicating in a foreign country. The entries from **The International Gesture Dictionary** will help you to do that.

BEFORE YOU READ

PREREADING ACTIVITIES

1. Make a list of some gestures that are commonly used in your country. For example, what do you do to show that something is too expensive? How do you express that you are full?

_____

_____

_____

_____

_____

2. Choose one gesture and demonstrate it to a small group of your classmates, who will try to guess what it means. You might need to ask another student or the teacher to help you with your demonstration.

3. Share and discuss your list with the rest of the class.

International Gesture Dictionary

R O G E R   A X T E L L

1 **Eyebrow Raise:** In Tonga, a gesture meaning "yes" or "I agree." In Peru, means "money" or "Pay me."

2 **Blink:** In Taiwan, blinking the eyes at someone is considered impolite.

3 **Wink:** Winking at women, even to express friendship, is considered improper in Australia.

4 **Eyelid Pull:** In Europe and some Latin American countries, means "Be alert" or "I am alert."

5 **Ear Grasp:** Grasping one's ears is a sign of repentance or sincerity in India. A similar gesture in Brazil— holding the lobe of one's ear between thumb and forefinger— signifies appreciation.

6 **Nose Tap:** In Britain, secrecy or confidentiality. In Italy, a friendly warning.

7 **Nose Thumb:** One of Europe's most widely known gestures, signifying mockery. May be done double-handed for greater effect.

8 **Nose Wiggle:** In Puerto Rico, "What's going on?"

9 **Cheek Screw:** Primarily an Italian gesture of praise.

10 **Cheek Stroke:** 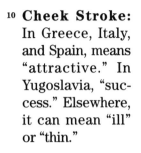In Greece, Italy, and Spain, means "attractive." In Yugoslavia, "success." Elsewhere, it can mean "ill" or "thin."

11 **Fingertips Kiss:** Common throughout Europe, particularly in Latin countries (and in Latin America). Connotes "aah, beautiful!," the object of which may be anything from a woman or a wine to a Ferrari or a soccer play. Origin probably dates to the custom of ancient Greeks and Romans who, when entering and leaving the temple, threw a kiss toward sacred objects such as statues and altars.

12 **Chin Flick:** "Not interested," "Buzz off," in Italy. In Brazil and Paraguay, "I don't know."

13 **Head Circle:** In most European and some Latin American countries, a circular motion of the finger around the ear means "crazy." In the Netherlands, it means someone has a telephone call.

14 **Head Nod:** In Bulgaria and Greece, signifies "no." In most other countries, "yes."

15 **Head Screw:** In Germany, a strong symbol meaning "You're crazy." Often used by drivers on the autobahn to comment on the driving skills of other travelers, this gesture can get you arrested! The same gesture is used in Argentina, but without the consequences.

16 **Head Tap:** In Argentina and Peru, "I'm thinking" or "Think." Elsewhere it can mean "He's crazy."

17 **Head Tilt**: In Paraguay, tilting the head backwards means "I forgot."

18 **Head Toss:** In southern Italy, Malta, Greece, and Tunisia, a negation. In Germany and Scandinavia, a beckoning motion. In India, "yes."

19 **One-Finger Point:** In most Middle and Far Eastern countries, pointing with the index finger is considered impolite. The open hand is used instead, or, in Indonesia, the thumb.

20 **Two-Finger Tap:** In Egypt, this means a couple is sleeping together and, true or false, is always rude. Can also mean, "Would you like to sleep together?"

21 **Thumbs Up:** In Australia, a rude gesture; in almost every other place in the world, simply means "okay."

22 **Flat-Hand Flick:** The universal flicking of the fingers toward the source of irritation, meaning "Go away" or "Get lost."

23 **Palm Push:** In Nigeria, pushing the palm of the hand forward with fingers spread is a vulgar gesture.

24 **Hand Purse:** Can signify a question or good or fear. Considered almost the national gesture of Italy.

25 **Hand Saw:** When you make a deal in Colombia and intend to share the profits, the gesture is one palm facing down with the other hand making a sawing motion across the back of the hand facing down.

26 **Hand Sweep:** In Latin America and the Netherlands, a sweeping or grabbing motion made toward your body, as though you were sweeping chips off a table, means that someone is stealing or "getting away with something." The same gesture in Peru means "money" or "Pay me."

27 **Waving:** Called the *moutza* in Greece, this is a serious insult, and the closer the hand to the other person's face, the more threatening it is considered. Same in Nigeria. Never use it to get a waiter's or cabdriver's attention. In Europe, raise the palm outward and wag the fingers in unison to wave "good-bye." Waving the whole hand back and forth can signify "no," while in Peru, that gesture means, "Come here."

28 **Height:** In Colombia and much of Latin America, only an animal's height is indicated by using the whole hand, palm down. It is polite to hold the palm facing the observer to show human height, or, in Mexico, to use the index finger.

29 The *Wai*: Traditional greeting in Thailand. Called the *namaste* in India.

30 Arms Fold: In Finland, folded arms are a sign of arrogance and pride. In Fiji, the gesture shows disrespect.

31 Elbow Tap: In Holland, "He's unreliable." In Colombia, "You are stingy."

32 The Fig: In some European and Mediterranean countries, an obscene gesture of contempt. In Brazil and Venezuela, a symbol of good luck reproduced in such diverse forms as paperweights and golden amulets worn around the neck.

● ●

HOW WELL DID YOU READ?

A. Which gestures would you use in the following situations?

1. You are in Italy, and you want to praise someone for doing a good job.

_____

2. You are in Brazil, and you want to show your roommate that you appreciate her cleaning the room.

_____

3. You are in Latin America at a soccer game. You've just seen your favorite player make the winning goal.

_____

4. You are in the Netherlands, and you want to tell your friend that she has a telephone call.

_____

5. You are in Thailand at a formal social gathering. The president of your university has just walked in the room. You need to greet him in the traditional way.

_____

FYI

Motorists are
required to drive
on the left side of
the road in 53
countries includ-
ing England,
Japan, Trinidad,
and Cyprus.

B. Misusing and misunderstanding gestures can cause confusion and embarrassment. Explain the confusion in the following situations.

1. You are at a restaurant in Taiwan, and you blink your eyes at the waitress while you are ordering. She gets angry.

_____

2. You are a tourist in Bulgaria. Your host offers you a drink. Since you are very thirsty, you nod your head. You are surprised when your host walks away without giving you a drink.

_____

3. You are eating dinner at your Australian friend's house. She asks you if you like her food. You give her the thumbs up sign. She becomes offended.

_____

4. You are a European visiting Peru. Your Peruvian friend asks you if you need help with some work you are doing. You wave your hand back and forth, then wonder why she comes over to you.

_____

APPLICATION OF INFORMATION

A. Here is a list of various gestures used in the United States. Some of them have more than one meaning. Find out at least one meaning for each gesture, and write an example of a situation when it might be used. You may interview people outside the classroom or ask your classmates if they know the meanings.

1. **cross your fingers**

   meaning: _____

   situation: _____

2. **wink**

   meaning: _____

   situation: _____

3. **shrug your shoulders**

meaning: _____

situation: _____

4. **stick your tongue out**

meaning: _____

situation: _____

5. **whistle**

meaning: _____

situation: _____

6. **snap your fingers**

meaning: _____

situation: _____

7. **clap your hands**

meaning: _____

situation: _____

8. **make a cross over your heart**

meaning: _____

situation: _____

B. What gestures do you use in your culture in these situations? Demonstrate them to your classmates.

1. to say that someone is crazy

2. to say "Come here"

3. to show that you've got a headache

4. to answer "I don't know"

5. to show that you are annoyed

6. to indicate that someone is cheap

7. to show that something is expensive

8. to say that you can't hear something

The Bean Cake and the Broom is an autobiographical story about an American woman, Dee Worman, who lived in Japan. The story shows that eating and cooking in a foreign place can sometimes be a confusing or an embarrassing—but always a memorable—experience.

Getting used to new kinds of food and eating habits is a big part of adjusting to a new culture. Anyone who has ever traveled, worked, or studied abroad has at least one story to tell about an experience with food.

1. Share a personal story with your classmates about your experience with foreign food or eating in a foreign country. Is your story about an experience that was embarrassing, funny, or unpleasant?

2. Make a list of adjectives to describe the food of your native culture. Try to think of at least ten words. Write your lists on the board and compare them.

3. What is the most unusual food you've ever eaten in a foreign country? What do you find strange about it?

4. Think about the eating habits in your native country. What similarities and differences have you noticed between the ones in your country and those in the United States or any other country you have visited?

5. What is your favorite American food? Your least favorite?

The article is presented in four parts. Read each part and do the comprehension check following it.

The Bean Cake and the Broom

DEE A. WORMAN
for Stephano Brocco

---------------- **PART 1** ----------------

1 he main problem for me, an American in Japan, was that I was always hungry. But not because of food shortages. Japan has plenty of food. It's just that the portions seemed so small.

2 My Japanese husband, Hiroshi, always maintained his weight. True, he was a martial artist and exercised a lot, but so did I. Still, whenever we went out to eat, I came home hungry. Satisfied always with his meal, Hiroshi was never hungry after dinner. I, however, would come home, pick through the refrigerator, and come up with some cheese or butter for a piece of bread. Hiroshi thought these Western foods were tasteless. He never drank milk or ate cheese or butter. He liked rice. Rice and fish or rice and tofu and vegetables. I liked those foods, too; in fact, I almost always cooked them, but I also had to have that extra piece of bread, or cheese, or bread and butter, or a Japanese pastry, filled with rich bean paste.

3 Hiroshi and I ran a gymnasium for *aikido*, a martial art of Japan, and Hiroshi often had to take part in dinners with his *aikido* colleagues. Sometimes I had to go along on these dinners. They were usually outside of the home, in a restaurant or a sushi bar. The people who paid were the hosts. It was a rather nice custom, I thought. And it means that the wives don't have to cook all the time, I remember thinking.

4 When there were women at the table, I watched how they ate. Putting a lot of food between two chopsticks is both impossible and bad table manners. Besides, the women never seemed to eat much. Men gobbled down huge bowls of rice and showed their appreciation with noises, but the women ate soundlessly. The custom, followed by some, of putting one's hand over one's mouth to hide the chewing movement of the lips, I found pleasant but time-consuming. It was dinner time and I was hungry. The pleasure and the atmosphere of the meal were initially lost on me. Also, like a bull in a china closet, I sometimes broke a delicately painted dish. I knew I had to shape up if I was to be a good Japanese wife.

5   Occasionally, we were asked to eat in someone's home. Usually that person, a man who was about the same rank in the martial arts as Hiroshi, would invite us and his wife would prepare and serve the meal. These dinners made me a little nervous because I wasn't sure of my role. I, too, practiced the martial arts, but at a somewhat lower rank. I was also the wife. As I learned more Japanese and got used to drinking more sake, I became more talkative. My pleasantries were fine, but I should learn to keep my opinions for when we were home, alone.

HOW WELL DID YOU READ?

A. Answer the following questions.

1. What was the narrator's main problem in Japan?

_____

2. What usually happened after Dee and Hiroshi came home from a meal out?

_____

3. What did Hiroshi and Dee do for a living?

_____

4. Why was Dee often nervous at social dinners?

_____

5. What differences did Dee mention between the way men and women eat in Japan?

_____

──────────── **PART 2** ────────────

6   The food at these dinners was always magnificent. Five or six different dishes were often prepared. Sake was abundant and little sweet and sour pickles were always on hand. I knew after a few of these dinners that I would soon have to prepare one.

7   That scared me. I wasn't a bad cook, even though Japanese food is an art to prepare, and I had some beautifully patterned dishes, but I didn't know how to act. I hadn't perfected my wife role yet. I was known to disagree at the table, something unheard of at a small dinner party. I was afraid that after cooking everything, I would want to go upstairs to our studio and take a nap or read a book or smoke a cigarette, or do all three. I knew that I would have to be a gracious hostess.

8 Hiroshi told me a week in advance that his friends, the Hondas, were coming for lunch. Mr. and Mrs. Honda and their son, five-year-old Isao, would be our guests. I liked the boy and was glad that he was going to come.

9 "Fine," I said to Hiroshi in Japanese. "I'd be happy to have your friends to lunch," and I immediately began thinking about the menu.

10 As if he could read my mind, Hiroshi said, "Nothing too elaborate, it's just a simple lunch and we all have to get back to work."

11 Lunch. Good. I could do lunch. And then I thought of ordering out for sushi. A lot of wives did that and it was always delicious. But I thought Hiroshi actually wanted to show off how his American wife could cook Japanese food. He would never say so, but I knew he liked a lot of my meals and I sometimes enjoyed just cooking all day and eating whatever I wanted without anybody watching. I would do lunch. In a week.

12 The next morning I started looking through my cookbooks and then remembered my favorite one: *Homestyle Japanese Cooking in Pictures* by Sadako Kohno, a 78-year-old Japanese woman who had cooked professionally for 50 years. She had also lived in New York City for 16 years and the recipes were in Japanese and English. I looked through the book wondering how many stores and markets I would have to enter to secure the ingredients. Then I came upon a beautiful picture: it was entitled, "Clear Soup with Flower-Shaped Prawn" (Hana-ebi no Sumashi-jiru) and showed a black lacquer bowl with a thin rim of gold around the outer edge. Floating inside the clear soup broth was a flower-shaped piece of shrimp surrounded artfully by shitake mushrooms, one stalk of asparagus, and one orange rind. There were not many ingredients and the directions seemed simple enough if I could cut the prawn correctly. . . .

13 I would try. I would make flowered prawns. My cat would enjoy eating my mistakes.

14 The rest of the menu came to me at different times all through the week. I read a little more, I sampled foods in department stores, and finally I came up with a menu.

15 We would have the prawn-decorated soup, trout grilled with salt, string beans with *goma* (sesame) sauce, and rice with green peas. For dessert we would have tea and bean cakes with red bean paste inside.

HOW WELL DID YOU READ?

B. Read the following statements. If a statement is true, write *T* on the line. If it is false, write *F*.

_____ 1. Dee was worried about preparing a Japanese meal for guests.

_____ 2. She was afraid that her cooking skills weren't good enough.

_____ 3. Dee decided on a lunch menu for her guests very quickly.

——— PART 3 ———

16   The day of the event loomed near. I scrubbed the small space of kitchen floor several times and washed down the sliding lucite and wood door that separated the kitchen from the larger space—the dining room.

17   I rose at 7:00 A.M. the day of the lunch and began cutting and washing the vegetables. I had gone to the markets the day before, but I still needed the bean paste cakes, which could be purchased fresh and warm at the corner vendor.

18   I noticed a slight autumn chill in the air as I walked home from the bean cake vendor. I wondered at the last minute if I was preparing appropriate foods for this season. My bag of bean cakes felt warm against my chest. There would be five of us in all . . . me, Hiroshi, Mr. and Mrs. Honda, and their son, Isao. I had bought ten bean cakes. Way too many, I thought, as I lifted a nice fat warm one out of the bag and began to eat it—feeling the thick bean paste on the first bite.

19   The guests arrived while I was at the stove. I had the kitchen door closed so that my cooking mess couldn't be seen from the dining area. I quietly opened and then closed the door behind, made my welcomes, and then offered the Hondas slippers and the best cushions around the low table on the straw *tatami* floor. Mrs. Honda presented me with a lovely gift box of *sembei* rice crackers. I was suddenly very happy to be the hostess this time.

20   After I poured the tea and the two beers for the men, I brought out the first course, carefully closing the door behind me. Mrs. Honda promptly exclaimed over the soup and even Mr. Honda looked interested. He knew me from *aikido* practice, we were often on the mats together, but he had no idea I was such "a fine Japanese cook," he said, emphasizing the word *Japanese*.

21   I did not kneel down to eat at the table with them because I had to go back into the small kitchen area and get the next dishes ready.

HOW WELL DID YOU READ?

C. Read the following statements. If a statement is true, write *T* on the line. If it is false, write *F*.

_____ 1. Dee had bought everything to prepare the lunch in advance.

_____ 2. She realized that she hadn't bought enough bean cakes.

_____ 3. Dee was pleased when she received a gift from Mrs. Honda.

_____ 4. The Hondas seemed impressed with Dee's cooking skills.

_____ 5. Dee was able to sit down and eat lunch with her guests.

─── **PART 4** ───

22   I put the grilled trout on the table and the string beans with *goma* sauce. Everyone was happily eating and Mrs. Honda was serving the tea and pouring the beer. I went back into the kitchen area, closed the door, and began to mix the fresh green peas into the warm rice when suddenly I felt another pang of hunger for a bean cake. They were all eating, and I hadn't had a thing since the last bean cake several hours earlier. I grabbed a bean cake from the bag and began chewing it greedily. A big glob of the thick red bean paste dropped down the front of my white shirt and continued to ooze down my shirt. Suddenly the door slid open and Isao stood staring alternately at me with the bean paste running down my blouse and the piece of bean cake I was still chewing. In fact, everyone was watching.

23   The boy started whining for his own bean cake. His mother, feeling embarrassed, came and dragged him back to his seat. I quickly shut the door, too embarrassed to even bring out the rice.

24   Hiroshi quietly opened and closed the door as I was trying to wash the bean paste out of my shirt. The two of us could hardly fit in the small kitchen space.

25   "Oh, Hiroshi, I'm so embarrassed. Look at me! How can I go back out there with this big red stain on my shirt?" I cried.

26   He began to laugh, but then thought better of it. "Just bring out the rice. I'll help you and then they'll leave."

27   "Leave? How do you know they'll leave?" I asked. They had only been seated around the table for 30 minutes.

28   "Because of an old Osaka country trick."

29   "What?" Perhaps I hadn't understood him. Hiroshi spoke almost no English and my Japanese was still limited.

30   He said slowly, "I'll put the broom upside down in the dining room. The Hondas will know when they see it that it is time for them to leave. It will be okay."

31   Again, I wasn't sure I had understood, so I repeated, "The old broom?" He nodded. "Upside down in the dining room? Where they are eating?" He nodded again. "And they'll leave? Really?" Another affirmative nod.

32   Hiroshi winked at me, opened the partition doors and even helped serve the rice. I looked down in embarrassment at the table as Mrs. Honda quietly poured the tea. When I finally looked up, the broom was indeed propped upside down against the left wall of the dining area. Out of the corner of my eye, I also noticed that Isao was still staring at me.

33   Not five minutes later, the Hondas rose and began to thank me for the wonderful lunch. It was such a pity that everyone had to get back to work. Isao began to cry again.

34   I raced into the kitchen, leaving open the partition, and grabbed the bag with the remaining bean cakes. Isao had followed me into the kitchen.

35   "Here, all for you," I chuckled, holding out the bag to him.

36   "Mine," he squealed, grabbing the bag and looking up at me with his sparkling five-year-old eyes. I laughed hard, bent down, and hugged him carefully so as not to squish the bean paste against him.

37   "Funny wife," he said.

● ●

HOW WELL DID YOU READ?

Answer the following questions.

1. What did Isao see when he opened the door to the kitchen?

_____

_____

2. Why was Dee embarrassed?

_____

_____

3. Why was Mrs. Honda embarrassed?

_____

_____

4. Why did Hiroshi suggest putting a broom upside down in the dining room?

_____

_____

ORGANIZING INFORMATION

Here is a list of events in the story. Put them in the correct time order by numbering them from 1 to 8.

_____ a. Dee spilled red bean paste on her white shirt.

_____ b. Hiroshi put a broom upside down in the dining room.

_____ c. Isao saw the bean cakes and started to cry.

_____ d. The Hondas left after quickly finishing their lunch.

_____ e. Hiroshi told Dee that he had invited his friends for lunch.

_____ f. Dee spent a week preparing for the lunch.

_____ g. The Hondas arrived and enjoyed the first part of their meal.

_____ h. Dee bought the bean cakes for the lunch.

EXPANDING VOCABULARY

For each of the following words, quickly read the paragraph cited (the number in parentheses) to find a word or phrase with the same meaning as the word(s) below.

1. contented (¶2) _____

2. devoured (¶4) _____

3. position (¶5) _____

4. plentiful (¶6) _____

5. available (¶6) _____

6. pleasant (¶7) _____

7. fancy (¶10) _____

8. tried, tasted (¶14) _____

9. cleaned (¶16) _____

10. woke up (¶17) _____

11. seller (¶18) _____

12. correct (¶18) _____

13. pillows (¶19) _____

14. ashamed (¶23) _____

15. shining (¶36) _____

BUILDING VOCABULARY SKILLS

PREFIXES

A *prefix* is a group of letters added at the beginning of a word to modify or change the meaning of the original word. If you know some commonly used prefixes, it will be easier for you to figure out the meanings of some unfamiliar words.

Here are some examples of words with prefixes from the story you have just read.

Examples

*Putting a lot of food between two chopsticks is both **impossible** and bad table manners.*

*These dinners made me a little nervous because I was **unsure** of my role.*

*I was known to **disagree** at the table, something **unheard** of at a small dinner party.*

All these prefixes, *im-*, *un-*, and *dis-*, mean *no* or *not*. They change the meaning of the original word to its opposite. For example, *impossible* means *not possible, unsure* means *not sure*, and *disagree* means *not to agree*. Other prefixes with this meaning include *il-*, *non-*, and *in-*.

Using these prefixes, write the opposite of each word listed below. You may need to use your dictionary.

1. interesting _____

2. logical _____

3. respectful _____

4. necessary _____

5. frequent _____

6. advantage _____

7. threatening _____

8. legal _____

9. appear _____

10. polite _____

11. pleasant _____

12. sense _____

13. appropriate _____

14. literate _____

APPLICATION OF INFORMATION

MAKING COMPARISONS

Make comparisons between the eating habits in your country and those in the United States. Discuss the time, place, menu, and social aspects associated with mealtime.

1. **breakfast**

   United States: _____

   _____

   your country: _____

   _____

2. **lunch**

   United States: _____

   _____

   your country: _____

   _____

3. **dinner**

   United States: _____

   _____

   your country: _____

   _____

4. **snacking**

   United States: _____

   _____

   your country: _____

   _____

Unscramble the letters below to discover words used in this unit. Write each word in the space provided. Then check your answers in the Answer Key on page 213.

1. isks

— ◯ — —

2. turseges

— — — ◯ — — — —

3. omorb

— ◯ — —

4. risttou

— ◯ — — — —

5. finsf

— ◯ — — ◯

6. ronujla

— ◯ — — — ◯ —

7. stucom

— — — — — ◯

8. ertungais

— ◯ — ◯ — — — — —

You will notice that eleven of the letters are circled. Write the circled letters in the spaces below. Then unscramble them to find a word about this book.

___ ___ ___ ___ ___ ___ ___ ___ ___ ___

9. _____

POSTREADING DISCUSSION QUESTIONS

1. Americans have an expression that says, "When in Rome, do as the Romans do." What do you think this means? Do you agree or disagree with this expression? Do you think it is always important to behave the way the natives do when you visit their country? Do you have a similar expression in your language?

   _____

2. Think about the changes in the way we live now as opposed to the way people lived fifty or a hundred years ago. With the ease of travel and the improvements in communications that have made the world a much smaller place, how have our impressions about other cultures changed?

READER'S JOURNAL

After you finish each unit in this book, you will write for approximately ten to twenty minutes in the space provided. This is called a reader's journal. You should feel free to use it to respond and react to the readings in a personal way and write about whatever you want. The purpose of this journal is to help you think about, tie together, and make sense of the readings you have just finished.

Before you write, you might want to think about the uses of gestures and the importance of customs. Then turn the page and begin writing.

READER'S JOURNAL

Date: _____

PLAYING TO WIN

FYi
Unit·2

Selections

Many people all over the world enjoy sports. Some enjoy sports as entertainment, others as a form of exercise or for the spirit of competition. This unit contains articles about people who play sports at the highest levels.

Think about and then discuss the following questions.

1. Most people enjoy watching, participating in, reading about, or discussing sports. Which of the above are true for you? Which sports do you enjoy?

2. Do you prefer team sports or individual sports? Why?

3. When you were growing up, which sports were you interested in? Did you ever dream about playing that sport professionally or competing in the Olympics? Did you have a favorite player or team that you followed? Do you now?

4. Who do you think is the world's greatest athlete? In addition to talent, what qualities should a good athlete have?

In **Looking Back**, Hakeem Olajuwon, a famous NBA (National Basketball Association) player, talks about himself. Hakeem is such a good basketball player that he is known as "Hakeem the Dream." In fact, in 1994 and 1995, Hakeem was voted the Most Valuable Player (MVP) in the NBA. The article talks about his growing up in Nigeria and coming to the United States on a basketball scholarship to the University of Houston.

BEFORE YOU READ

PREREADING QUESTIONS

Look at the Bio-Map on p. 33.

1. Where has Hakeem lived and played basketball?

2. What are some of the highlights of his life? How do you think the information in the article will be organized?

Looking Back

H A K E E M   O L A J U W O N

Hakeem Olajuwon, age 29, of the Houston Rockets is one of the NBA's best centers. He is a seven-time All-Star, and he has averaged 22.9 points and 12.5 rebounds per game in his professional career. The seven-foot Hakeem recently talked about what it was like to grow up in the African country of Nigeria.

1   grew up in a huge city called Lagos. My family lived in a three-bedroom house there.

2   Lagos, which is the capital of Nigeria, has a population of 1.2 million people. Mainly because of the area's oil industry, people from all over the world work and live in Lagos.

3   I was the third oldest of six children (five boys and a girl). My father, Salaam, and my mother, Abike, taught all of us the importance of hard work. My parents had jobs buying and selling cement.

4   My mother and father were loving but strict. They made sure we were respectful of other adults. In Nigeria, if you're impolite to adults, they can punish you, even if they aren't your parents.

5   My father loved sports, but he didn't want me to put sports ahead of education. Still, I started playing soccer, the most popular sport in Nigeria, when I was four. I didn't play basketball at all.

6   I went to a boarding school[1] from ages 12 to 17. My schoolmates came from different Nigerian tribes. Each tribe speaks its own regional language, so Nigerians learn English to communicate with one another. Having friends from many backgrounds taught me to appreciate and respect the differences among people.

7   In high school, I played soccer and field hockey. Also, I was a pretty good high jumper and a star in team handball.

8   One day when I was 16, coach Oscar Johnson from the Nigerian national basketball team came up to me during soccer practice. I guess I was the only 6' 9" soccer goalie he had ever seen! He persuaded me to give basketball a try.

9   Coach Johnson took me to a court, shot a few baskets, and then passed me the ball. My first shot missed the basket completely. I said, "Let me try again!"

10   Coach Johnson worked with me on shooting, and when I made my first basket, I didn't want to stop. Before long, we had shot baskets for two hours!

11   I fell in love with basketball that day, and I worked hard to improve my game. My efforts paid off. Later that year, I made the national team. Even though I was only 16, I was put on the team so that I could learn the rules. I never dreamed that I would play in the NBA. I hoped to go to an American college someday, but I didn't know how or when I would do it.

1 boarding school   A private high school where students live at the school.

12   The opportunity came in 1980, when I received a basketball scholarship to the University of Houston. The coach had heard about me from a friend of his who coached the Central African junior national team. I've lived in Houston ever since. Three of my brothers have also moved to the U.S. Two of them play basketball at the University of Texas at San Antonio.

13   Though Houston is now my home, I'm thankful for the lessons I learned and the fun I had growing up in Nigeria. . . .

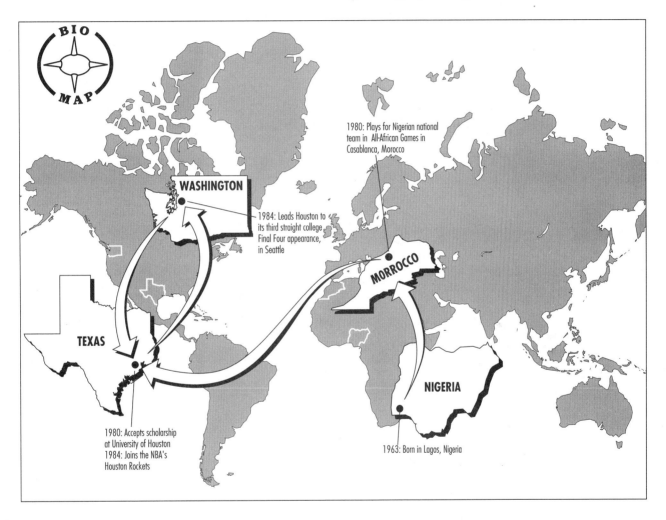

BIO MAP

WASHINGTON

1984: Leads Houston to
its third straight college
Final Four appearance,
in Seattle

TEXAS

1980: Accepts scholarship
at University of Houston
1984: Joins the NBA's
Houston Rockets

1980: Plays for Nigerian national
team in All-African Games in
Casablanca, Morocco

MORROCCO

NIGERIA

1963: Born in Lagos, Nigeria

A. Read the following statements. If a statement is true, write *T* on the line. If it is false, write *F*.

_____ 1. Hakeem grew up in a small desert village in Nigeria.

_____ 2. Respect is an important value in Nigeria.

_____ 3. All Nigerians speak the same native language.

_____ 4. Basketball was always Hakeem's favorite sport.

_____ 5. Hakeem made the national basketball team when he was only sixteen years old.

_____ 6. Hakeem now considers Houston his home.

B. Circle the letter of the word or phrase that best completes each sentence.

1. People from all over the world live in Lagos because _____.
   a. it is the capital of Nigeria
   b. it is in the desert
   c. of its oil industry
   d. of its central location

2. Hakeem grew up _____.
   a. learning the importance of hard work
   b. learning respect for others
   c. playing sports
   d. *(all of the above)*

3. As a young child, Hakeem played _____.
   a. soccer
   b. basketball
   c. field hockey
   d. handball

4. Nigerians learn English _____.
   a. because it is the native language
   b. so they can attend American schools
   c. to communicate with each other
   d. *(none of the above)*

5. Hakeem played basketball for _____.
   a. the Nigerian national team
   b. the University of Houston
   c. the NBA
   d. *(all of the above)*

ORGANIZING INFORMATION

Here is a list of some important events in Hakeem Olajuwon's life. Put them in the correct time order by numbering them from 1 to 7.

_____ a. Hakeem made the national team.

_____ b. He moved to Houston.

_____ c. He was born in Lagos, Nigeria.

_____ d. At the age of four, Hakeem started playing soccer.

_____ e. He went to boarding school.

_____ f. Hakeem received a scholarship to the University of Houston.

_____ g. He tried basketball for the first time with Coach Johnson.

FIGURE IT OUT

VOCABULARY IN CONTEXT

Without using your dictionary, write an approximate definition or a synonym for the highlighted words in the following sentences.

1. *Lagos, the capital of Nigeria, has a **population** of 1.2 million people.*

   _____

2. *They made sure we were **respectful** of other adults. In Nigeria, if you're impolite to adults, they can punish you, even if they aren't your parents.*

   _____

3. *My schoolmates came from different Nigerian tribes. Each tribe speaks its own **regional** language, so Nigerians learn English to communicate with one another.*

   _____

4. *I guess I was the only 6'9" soccer goalie he had ever seen! He **persuaded** me to give basketball a try.*

   _____

5. *My efforts **paid off**. Later that year, I made the national team.*

   _____

6. *The **opportunity** came in 1980, when I received a basketball scholarship.*

   _____

Following a Dream is about several professional athletes who have moved from one country to another to advance their careers. In these short biographies, the athletes talk about what it was like to move to a new country and start their lives over again.

The athletes you are going to read about in the first part moved to the United States from other countries. As you read these paragraphs, think about each athlete's impressions of the United States.

Following a Dream

MARTINA NAVRATILOVA

Tennis Star. Born: Czechoslovakia

1   When Navratilova was 16 she went to Florida to play in a tennis tournament. She had never been in the U.S. before. "The thing I remember the most is oranges and coconuts lying on the ground and nobody picking them up!" Martina says. Fresh oranges and coconuts, like many other things, were almost impossible to get in Czechoslovakia.

2   Navratilova has lived in the U.S. since 1975. She says the U.S. isn't perfect—there is too much discrimination here against people who are different. But she loves America and its bold spirit. "Americans don't get discouraged easily. If they believe in something, they go after it," she says.

CHRISTIAN OKOYE

Running back, Kansas City Chiefs. Born: Nigeria

3   When Okoye moved to the United States at the age of 21, he found out that a lot of Americans don't know much about the rest of the world. Some people he met thought Nigeria was an island near Florida!

4   Okoye came on a track and field scholarship to Azusa Pacific University in California. In college, he threw the discus and hammer, and he played football for the first time.

5   At first, Okoye didn't know the rules, but he worked hard and became one of the best running backs in football. He stayed in the U.S. to play in the NFL, and in 1990 he married an American woman.

6   Okoye says Americans don't appreciate how lucky they are: "They don't understand how people in other countries are suffering, hoping they could have the same opportunities that Americans have."

JOSE SANTOS

Jockey. Born: Chile

7   When Santos was 17, he watched a tape of American jockey Steve Cauthen (see page 43) winning the Kentucky Derby. Santos started thinking how great it would be to ride—and live—in the U.S.

8   Santos moved to the U.S. six years later. He worked hard and became one of the top riders at New York tracks. "When I started paying taxes, I felt like an American," he says.

9   The only thing Santos doesn't like is the prejudice he sees. Recently, a man angrily told him that Spanish-speaking immigrants, like Santos, get good jobs that ought to go to people born in the U.S. Says Santos: "I explained to him that in this country there is opportunity for everybody, if you want to work."

SANDRA FARMER-PATRICK

Hurdler. Born: Jamaica

10   When Farmer-Patrick was 9, her family sent her to New York City to live with her grand aunt. They sent her to the U.S. because there was more opportunity here.

11   Farmer-Patrick took up track in junior high school. But her grand aunt wouldn't let her wear running shorts because her Pentecostal religion forbids women to wear shorts or pants. Sandra had to run wearing a skirt!

12   Farmer-Patrick earned a track and field scholarship to California State University at Los Angeles. In 1988, she married U.S. hurdler David Patrick. Last summer, competing for the U.S. at the Barcelona Olympics, she won a silver medal in the 400-meter hurdles.

13   Farmer-Patrick feels that coming to the U.S. was a blessing. "Every little child in Jamaica dreams of coming to the United States," she says.

JULIO FRANCO

Second Baseman, Texas Rangers. Born: Dominican Republic

14   When Franco was 16, he came to the U.S. to play minor league baseball. He spoke only Spanish, and

the only foods he knew how to order in English were fried chicken and French fries. "I ate those foods for three months," he says.

15 Franco was the American League batting champion in 1991. After the season, he became a U.S. citizen. "This country gave me the chance to become a great ballplayer and the right to be an American," he says.

16 Franco wishes kids in the U.S. would show more respect for their elders. "In the Dominican Republic, I don't care how old you are," says Franco, "you listen to your parents. I *still* listen to my mother!"

BRIAN QUINN

Midfielder, U.S. Soccer Team.
Born: Northern Ireland

17 When Quinn was 20, he moved to the U.S. to play for the Los Angeles Aztecs of the North American Soccer League. He was surprised by the variety of food in the U.S. "You have 30 or 40 different kinds of fish!" he says. "In Ireland when we had fish, my mother would ask, 'What kind of fish do you want today, brown or white?'"

18 Quinn now lives in Poway, California, with his wife and six kids. In 1991, while he was playing for the San Diego Sockers, he was sworn in as a U.S. citizen during halftime of a Socker home game.

19 "A lady from the immigration service gave me a certificate and a flag," says Quinn. "Then a military band played 'God Bless the U.S.A.' It was incredible. The whole stadium stood up!"

GARY ANDERSON

Placekicker, Pittsburgh Steelers.
Born: South Africa

20 Anderson and his parents came to America when Gary was 18. His parents left South Africa because they didn't like the South African government's policy of apartheid. Apartheid separates blacks and whites and does not give blacks equal rights.

21 Anderson and his family settled in Downingtown, Pennsylvania. The second day there, Anderson took some footballs to the high school field to see if he could kick them the way he had kicked rugby and soccer balls all his life. Anderson had never touched an American football before.

22 The high school football coach happened to see Anderson kicking. He was impressed. He told Anderson he knew the coach of the Philadelphia Eagles and could arrange a tryout. At the tryout the next day, Anderson kicked a 50-yard field goal on his very first try! Four college coaches were at the tryout. They each offered Anderson football scholarships to their colleges on the spot. Anderson chose Syracuse University in upstate New York.

23 Anderson is now one of the best placekickers in NFL history. He and his wife and two sons live in Pittsburgh, Pennsylvania. "People don't think about Americans favorably overseas," Anderson says. "Nobody likes the biggest [country]. But Americans are the most kind people in the world."

**A. Complete the following chart with the athletes' impressions of the
   United States.**

Athletes	Their Impressions	Your Impressions
Martina Navratilova		
Christian Okoye		
Jose Santos		
Sandra Farmer-Patrick		
Julio Franco		
Brian Quinn		
Gary Anderson		

FYi

In the 1994
World Cup, a
total of fifty-two
soccer matches
were played in
over forty days, in
four time zones,
with a cumulative
audience of 32
billion people.

**B. How do the athletes' impressions of the United States compare
   with your own? Write your impressions in the above chart.**

39

REMEMBERING DETAILS

Match the athletes with their sports.

Sports	Athletes
_____ 1. tennis	a. Brian Quinn
_____ 2. baseball	b. Gary Anderson
_____ 3. horse racing	c. Julio Franco
_____ 4. football	d. Sandra Farmer-Patrick
_____ 5. hurdles	e. Jose Santos
_____ 6. soccer	f. Christian Okoye
	g. Martina Navratilova

SCANNING FOR DETAILS

Scanning is a technique that helps you locate information in an article quickly. You should use this method when you are looking for the answer to a specific question. When you scan, your eyes move quickly across the printed lines, but without reading every word. As you scan, try to look for key information that you need in order to answer the questions. For example, if a question asks you to find an age or a date, look for a number. As soon as you find the information you want, move on to the next question.

Scan the article to find out the answers to the following questions. To help you with the first two questions, clues are provided. For the other questions, decide what key information you will scan for, and write the clue in the space provided.

A golf ball can go as fast as 165 miles per hour.

1. What was the average age of the athletes when they came to the United States? (CLUE: Look for numbers that indicate ages.)

_____

2. Which three athletes won scholarships to American universities? (CLUE: Look for the names of universities.)

_____

3. Name two athletes who married Americans. (CLUE: _____.)

_____

4. Who feels that American kids are disrespectful?

(CLUE: _____)

_____

5. Who was the American League batting champion in 1991?

(CLUE: _____)

_____

6. Who won a silver medal in the 400-meter hurdles at the Barcelona Olympics? (CLUE: _____)

_____

DISTINGUISHING FACT FROM OPINION

Being able to tell the difference between fact and opinion is an important reading skill. A **fact** is something that happened or a statement that can be proven. An **opinion**, on the other hand, is someone's belief, feeling, or judgment.

Read each statement below. If you think a statement is a fact (something that can be proven), write *FC* on the line. If you think it is an opinion (someone's idea or assumption), write *OP*.

_____ 1. North Americans do not get discouraged easily.

_____ 2. There is too much prejudice in the United States.

_____ 3. Many athletes from other countries have come to America to play their sports.

_____ 4. American children do not show enough respect for older people.

_____ 5. There is a greater variety of fish in the United States than there is in Ireland.

_____ 6. Gary Anderson was offered a football scholarship by Syracuse University.

_____ 7. Americans are the kindest people in the world.

FYI

The top average speed for Winter Olympic sports is in downhill skiing—65 miles per hour.

All the athletes you have just read about moved to the United States from other countries. Now, you are going to read about two American athletes who left the United States to live abroad.

KONISHIKI AND STEVE CAUTHEN FOUND OPPORTUNITIES OVERSEAS.

Two Who Left America

1   Some U.S. athletes go overseas to play sports for a few months each year. In Europe, there are professional leagues for volleyball, soccer, and other sports. But most American athletes come home to the United States when their season ends.

2   Two U.S.-born athletes who have moved permanently to other countries are 580-pound sumo wrestler Konishiki of Japan and 115-pound jockey Steve Cauthen of England.

3   **Konishiki** was born with the name Salevaa Atisanoe on the Hawaiian island of Oahu. He played football in high school, but because of his huge size, he decided to take up the Japanese sport of sumo. He moved to Japan in 1982. The manager of the wrestlers with whom he trains gave him the sumo name of Konishiki.

4   Konishiki is the second non-Japanese champion in sumo history. He speaks Japanese, has a Japanese wife, and is becoming a Japanese citizen.

5   In Japan, Konishiki is still considered a foreigner by many

Japanese people. He often misses Hawaii. "I miss the food, my family, the sunshine, the beaches, and [American] TV and sports," he says.

6   Konishiki says that Japanese people work very hard and believe in doing what's best for the group or team. "In the U.S., it's a lot more individual," he says. "What you do is really up to you."

7   **Steve Cauthen** was born and raised in Walton, Kentucky. In 1978, he and a horse named Affirmed won the Triple Crown—the Kentucky Derby, the Preakness Stakes, and the Belmont Stakes.

8   But a year later, Cauthen was in a slump. He accepted an offer to move to Newmarket, England, and to ride for a trainer there.

9   Cauthen found it easy to adjust to his new home. "Life in England is country life," Cauthen says. "I feel as though I fit in well."

10   Cauthen was England's top jockey in 1984, 1985, and 1987. He recently married a woman he met there (she is from Kentucky too). Like Konishiki, Cauthen may stay in his adopted country until he retires. But, he still loves America.

11   "England's a big part of my life," Cauthen says, "but Kentucky's my home. Always will be."

● ●

RECALLING INFORMATION

How much can you remember? Complete the paragraph with information from the article. See how much you can do without referring to the article. Then go back and look up the rest of the answers.

Both Konishiki and Cauthen left the United States to live abroad.

Konishiki, who was born in _____, is a

_____ wrestler. He now lives in _____.

Steve Cauthen, from _____, is a _____.

He practices his sport in _____.

TALK IT OVER

DISCUSSION QUESTIONS

1. Can you think of any people who have moved to or from your country for their careers? Were they successful? Did any of them become famous? What is the difference between fame and success?

2. Would you ever want to work in another country? What do you think are the advantages and disadvantages of working in another country?

On Top of Her Game is about Michelle Akers, the best female soccer player in the world. Keep in mind that this article was written in 1993, which was before the World Cup came to the United States.

BEFORE YOU READ

PREREADING DISCUSSION

1. "To be on top" is an expression that means having mastery or control of something. Why do you think the article is entitled "On Top of Her Game"?

2. Although soccer has traditionally been a men's sport, women are also interested in watching and playing soccer. Do you think there is a place for women in professional soccer? Why or why not?

FIRST READING

Read the article one time quickly and complete the summary that follows with as many of the facts as you can remember.

● ●

On Top of Her Game

K E N T   H A N N O N

1   In 1994, the United States will host the World Cup soccer tournament. The World Cup is held only once every four years, and it's one of the world's biggest sports events.

2   As in the World Series[1] and the Super Bowl[2], only men play in the World Cup. That's too bad. Women play soccer, too, and they would love to have a hugely popular World Cup tournament of their own. They would love to get as much attention as the male players will in 1994.

3   "Our game is fast," says Michelle Akers, 26. "It's fun. And when more people see women playing soccer at this level, they are going to get hooked."

4   Michelle knows what she's talking about. She is a star forward on the world champion U.S. women's soccer team. Most experts believe she is the best female soccer player in the world.

5   Michelle is 5' 10" tall and weighs 150 pounds. It's easy to spot her on the field, even if you don't know her

[1] **World Series** Final baseball games played each fall in the United States and Canada to determine the best team.
[2] **Super Bowl** Final football games played each January to determine the best football team in the United States.

jersey number (10). When she rushes the net, her curly hair is whipped by the wind. As she dribbles the ball down the field, her legs are a blur. The ball seems connected to her feet with an invisible rubber band.

6   Michelle has won more international honors than any other player, female or male, in U.S. soccer history. She was an All-American four times at the University of Central Florida. In 1988, when Michelle was a senior, she was named college player of the year.

7   Although there is no World Cup in women's soccer, the first women's world championship tournament was held last November [1991], in Guangzhou, China. Led by Michelle, the U.S. team won the championship. It was the first time that any U.S. soc-cer team, women's or men's, had become the best in the world.

8   Sadly for the U.S. women, their victory didn't get much coverage in newspapers or on television. "How long do we have to wait before people discover that women's soccer, like women's tennis, is just as exciting as the men's game?" asks Michelle.

9   Michelle wishes the women's world championship were as popular as the men's World Cup. But she is thrilled that the World Cup tournament is coming to the U.S. because it will help make soccer more popular here. Soccer has never been as popular in the U.S. as it is in the rest of the world. One in five people in the world watched the World Cup in 1990— that's more than one billion people!

10   Michelle travels with the U.S. women's team for as many as eight months a year. Unlike members of the U.S. men's team, who earn from $30,000 to $60,000 per season, Michelle is not paid for playing on the national team. However, she does receive a salary from Tyresco F.C., the semi-pro team she plays for in Sweden four months a year.

11   Michelle grew up in Santa Clara, California. As a kid, she took swimming lessons and loved playing softball and other sports. "People still called girls like me 'tomboys' back then," says Michelle. "But I didn't care. I liked playing football with the guys in my neighborhood."

12   Michelle started playing soccer when she was 8 years old. Her hero was Pelé, the soccer star from Brazil. At first, she played goalie, and she cried every time her Police Athletic League team lost. "When you're the goalie," she says, "you think every loss is your fault."

13   Michelle practiced hard to improve her soccer skills. By age 10, she had become an excellent ball handler. Her coach would often start her at goalie and then switch her to center. Soon, her coach switched her position to center for good. "I love to juggle the ball from my feet to my thighs to my head," says Michelle. "I worked on those skills even when I was a goalie."

14   Michelle went on to become a star in high school. She joined the U.S. women's team in 1985, during the summer before her sophomore year at college.

15   Michelle says that her strongest weapon is her attitude. "I'll do anything to win," she says. Her strongest physical weapon is her thunderous kick, which she uses to pound the ball into the net.

16   "Most goals are kicked from the 18-yard box, which is 18 yards from the net," says Michelle. "I can score from as far away as 30 yards."

17   In 1988, Michelle attended a clinic run by the Dallas Cowboys'[3] kicking coach. She had never kicked a football before. A lot of people had told her that women couldn't kick field goals, but that just made her enjoy the challenge even more. At the clinic, she booted several 50-yard field goals. One football agent was so impressed that he urged her to spend part of her practice time booting a football instead of a soccer ball. He thought that Michelle could become the first female player in the history of the National Football League.

18   "He said, 'Don't you see how much money you could make?'" says Michelle. Though Michelle found placekicking interesting, she wanted to devote all her time to soccer.

19   Michelle always plays hard— sometimes too hard for her own good. It's surprising that she's still playing after seven knee operations, a concussion, two lost teeth, numerous stitches, and several black eyes.

20   "Lots of players never even get a bloody nose," says Michelle. "But if I see a loose ball in a crowd of players, I'll stick my body in there and try to come out with the ball. You name an injury, and I've had it."

21   "Michelle is courageous, and that makes her reckless," says Anson Dorrance, the coach of the U.S. women's team. "And when she lets fly with a kick, it's a nightmare for any defender or goalie."

22   Michelle says that her greatest thrill was helping the United States win the world championship last fall. She scored a team-high 10 goals in six tournament games. The championship game, against Norway, was played in front of 65,000 fans. Michelle scored the winning goal in the Americans' 2–1 victory.

23   "When I was a kid, I didn't have female soccer players to admire," says Michelle. "But by winning the world championship, my teammates and I have given something to young female soccer players that we never had as kids: someone to be like."

---

[3] **Dallas Cowboys** The football team located in Dallas, Texas.

RECALLING INFORMATION

How much can you remember? Complete the paragraph with information from the article. See how much you can fill in without referring to the article. Then go back and look up the rest of the answers.

Michelle Akers is the best _____ soccer player in the world. She plays star forward on the _____ women's soccer team. Michelle has won many national and international _____. In 1991, Michelle's team won the first women's world _____ tournament. According to Michelle, her strongest weapon is her _____. She says she will do anything to _____. In fact, she has suffered many injuries playing soccer.

SECOND READING

Now read the article again more carefully and answer the questions.

UNDERSTANDING ORGANIZATION

PARAGRAPHS

Most reading material is organized into paragraphs. All the information in a paragraph (¶) is related to one topic. Being able to identify the topic of a paragraph is a useful skill in reading comprehension.

Using paragraph numbers in the article, identify the one(s) that

1. describes what Michelle looks like ¶_____

2. lists her honors ¶_____

3. tells what she does during the year ¶_____

4. discuss her childhood ¶_____

5. describe her injuries ¶_____

6. talks about her greatest thrill ¶_____

Michelle is quoted directly several times in the article. Read each quotation and discuss its meaning using the questions as a guide.

1. *When I was a kid, I didn't have female soccer players to admire. But by winning the world championship, my teammates and I have given something to young female soccer players that we never had as kids: someone to be like.* Michelle says that she and her teammates have given girls role models, people to be like. Why do so many athletes become role models? Do you think all athletes make good role models? What qualities make someone a good role model?

2. *Our game is fast. It's fun. And when more people see women playing soccer at this level, they are going to get hooked.* What do you think "get hooked" means in this sentence? Why does Michelle think people will get hooked on women's soccer?

3. *How long do we have to wait before people discover that women's soccer, like women's tennis, is just as exciting as the men's game?* Based on this quote, which of the following statements do you think Michelle would agree with? Circle the appropriate letters.

   a. We have waited too long for people to appreciate women's soccer.
   b. We haven't waited long enough for women's soccer to become as popular as men's soccer.
   c. Women's soccer is just as exciting as men's soccer.
   d. Most people do not think women's tennis is very exciting.
   e. Women's soccer is as exciting as women's tennis.

1. Why do you think men's sports are more popular than women's sports? Do you think this will change in the future? Why or why not?

2. Do you think men are naturally better athletes? Explain your answer. Do you think men and women should play on the same teams?

3. What are some traditional women's sports?

4. Soccer is one of the most popular sports in the world. However, in 1314, King Edward II of England passed a law that forbade the playing of soccer: "There is a great noise caused by hustling over large balls from which many evils arise. We condemn and forbid on behalf of the King, on pain of punishment, such game to be used in the city of the future."[1] What kinds of "evils" do you think this law was referring to? Are these "evils" considered to be a problem today?

---

[1] Vick Braden and Louis Phillips, *Sportsathon* (New York: Puffin Books, 1986).

The title of this unit is "Playing to Win." The best-known athletic competition in the world is the Olympic Games. The Olympics bring together athletes from every corner of the world. The following article, **The Olympic Games**, presents basic information about the games.

BEFORE YOU READ

PREREADING ACTIVITIES

1. Make a list of the facts you know about the Olympics.

2. Listed below are facts about the history of the Olympics, but they are not in the correct order. Read them carefully, paying special attention to dates, transition words, pronoun references, and other clues. Put them in the correct time order by numbering them from 1 to 12.

_____ a. At first, they consisted of one competition, a 200-yard foot race.

_____ b. Women were first allowed to compete in 1900.

_____ c. It was a French educator, Baron Pierre de Coubertin, who had the idea of organizing a modern Olympics.

_____ d. The first Winter Olympic Games were held in 1924.

_____ e. The goal would be to encourage personal excellence and good feelings among countries.

_____ f. The first recorded Olympic Games were held in Olympia, Greece in 776 B.C.

_____ g. He felt that they were not appropriate for a Christian society.

_____ h. In the sixth century A.D., an earthquake destroyed the stadium in Olympia, and a landslide buried the ruins.

_____ i. The first modern Olympics were held in 1896 in Athens, Greece.

_____ j. The games were banned in the fourth century A.D. by Emperor Theodosius I, of Rome.

_____ k. The games in Athens included only those sports that are traditionally played in summer.

_____ l. In 1875, a group of German architects discovered the ruins.

There are many traditions and symbols associated with the Olympic Games. Read the information about them below and then discuss the questions that follow.

● ●

The Olympic Games

1 **Symbol:** The symbol of the Olympics, five circles that are linked together, represents good sportsmanship among all peoples. The rings also symbolize the five continents—Europe, Asia, Africa, Australia, and America. Each ring is a different color—blue, yellow, black, green, and red.

2 **Motto:** *Citius, Altius, Fortius* is Latin and means "faster, higher, braver." The motto was written by Father Didon, a French educator, in 1895.

3 **Creed:** "The most important thing in the Olympic Games is not to win but to take part, just as the most important thing in life is not the triumph but the struggle. The essential thing is not to have conquered but to have fought well."

4 **Oath:** At the opening ceremony of the Olympics, one of the athletes from the host country recites the following oath: "In the name of all competitors, I promise that we will take part in these Olympic Games, respecting and abiding by the rules which govern them, in the true spirit of sportsmanship, for the glory of sport and the honor of our teams." The oath and the creed were both written by Pierre de Coubertin, the founder of the modern Olympics.

5 **Flame:** The flame symbolizes the connection between the original and the modern games. The flame is carried from Olympia, Greece, to the site of the games by relays of thousands of runners. Planes and ships carry the flame across mountains and water. It continues to burn until the games are over.

6 **Opening Ceremony:** The opening ceremonies of the Olympic Games are very exciting. They begin with a parade of all the athletes into the stadium. The Greek athletes always go first in honor of the original Olympics. The other countries follow in alphabetical order. The government leader of the host country then announces that the games are open. Trumpets play, and cannons are fired as the Olympic flag is raised. Hundreds of doves are set free as a symbol of peace. The grand finale is a spectacular show performed by local artists.

TALK IT OVER

DISCUSSION
QUESTIONS

1. The five interlocking rings of the Olympics is one of the most well-known symbols in the world. What two things does the symbol represent? Why do you think this symbol is an appropriate representation of the Olympic Games?

2. The Olympic flag shows the symbol of the five rings. Describe your national flag. The fifty stars on the flag of the United States symbolize the fifty states in the union. The thirteen stripes represent the original thirteen colonies. What does your national flag symbolize?

3. A motto is a phrase or expression used to encourage action. How is the Olympic motto a guide to the participants in the games? The motto of the French Revolution was, "Liberty, Equality, Fraternity." What other mottoes can you think of?

4. A creed is a system of beliefs. According to the Olympic creed, what is the most important thing in the games? How does this relate to life in general? Do you agree with the message of the Olympic creed? Why or why not?

5. An oath is a pledge or promise. What do the athletes promise to do in the Olympics?

6. What does the flame symbolize?

7. The opening ceremonies are always very impressive. Have you ever seen the ceremonies in person? On television? In your opinion, what makes them so exciting?

Look at the charts below. They show the medal winnings of the twelve countries that won the largest number of medals in the modern Winter Olympics (before 1994 when the Soviet Union competed as one country). In groups, write questions based on the information in the charts. Then exchange your questions with other groups and write answers.

Example
What two countries received the same number of silver medals?

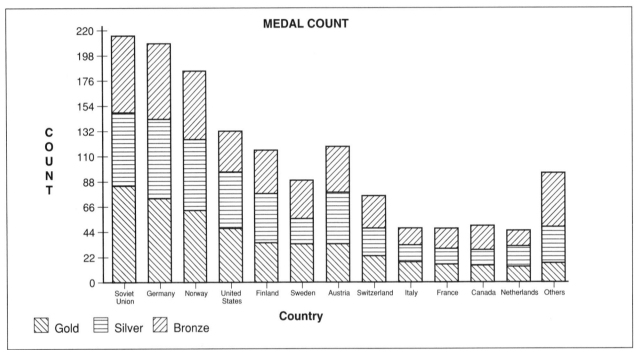

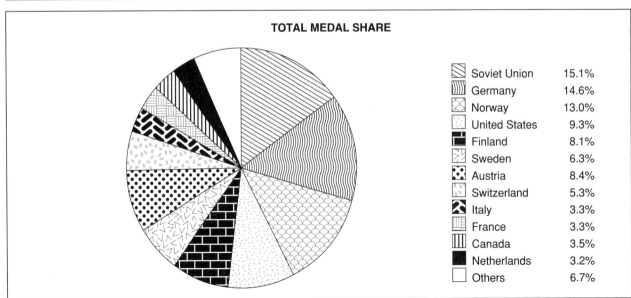

TALK IT OVER

DISCUSSION
QUESTIONS

1. What countries do you think are included in the group called "others"?

2. What additional countries compete in the Summer Olympics? What twelve countries do you think would be listed as winners for the summer games?

WORD FORMS

Complete the sentences with the correct word.

1. **popular, popularity, popularize, popularly**

    a. Women's soccer is gaining _____.

    b. It is _____ believed that men's soccer is more exciting than women's soccer.

    c. Soccer is a very _____ sport.

    d. Michelle and her teammates are helping to _____ women's soccer.

2. **nation, national, nationality, nationalize**

    a. The government wants to _____ the oil industry.

    b. Many _____ send teams to play in the World Cup.

    c. People of many different _____ participate in the Olympics.

    d. Hakeem made the _____ basketball team when he was only sixteen years old.

3. **immigrant, immigrate, immigration**

    a. Some people _____ to the United States to look for better jobs.

    b. The _____ laws are very complicated and it is often difficult for foreigners to understand them.

    c. Many of the excellent athletes in America are _____ .

(continued on the next page)

4. **athlete, athletics, athletic**

   a. Konishiki and Steve Cauthen are two American
      _____ who now live in other countries.

   b. Hakeem Olajuwon and Michelle Akers were both very
      _____ children.

   c. Our school stresses education as well as _____.

5. **compete, competitor, competition, competitive**

   a. Basketball teams in the United States are very _____.

   b. The top five _____ in the Grand Prix race are from
      Brazil.

   c. In order to _____ in the essay contest, you must be
      at least fifteen years old.

   d. There is a lot of _____ for the scholarship.

6. **educate, education, educational, educationally**

   a. She studied very hard in college and got a good _____.

   b. His parents prefer that he watch _____ programs.

   c. They were _____ at the best private schools.

   d. Some teaching methods are more _____ correct
      than others.

7. **communicate, communication, communicative, communicable**

   a. Television is one of the most important means of _____.

   b. Chicken pox is a _____ disease.

   c. She is a very interesting and _____ person.

   d. It is important for parents to _____ openly and
      honestly with their children.

1. In what ways are the Olympic games big business?

2. How do the Olympic games change the city that hosts them?

**SPORTS
EXPRESSIONS**

English speakers use many expressions taken from the world of sports.

A. Read the following paragraph and try to guess the meaning of the expressions in italics.

Leon and Justin are both running for class president. In order to get more votes, Leon started spreading rumors about Justin. Although the rumors were not true, Leon hoped the other students would *swallow them hook, line, and sinker.* One thing he said was that Justin wouldn't make a good class president because he was not a good athlete. Leon blamed the fact that their school had lost the basketball championship on Justin. He told people that Justin didn't have school spirit and wasn't a *team player.* Justin became very upset at Leon's tactics, which were *hitting below the belt.* In fact, Justin thought about *throwing in the towel.* But Justin's friends were *in his corner,* and they convinced him not to give up. In the end, he took their advice and decided to *go for the gold.* After considering *the odds,* Justin decided to stay in the race. He realized that most of the students would ignore Leon and think his tactics were *out in left field.*

B. Match the expressions with their meanings.

_____ 1. to swallow hook, line, and sinker

_____ 2. to be a team player

_____ 3. to hit below the belt

_____ 4. to throw in the towel

_____ 5. to be in his corner

_____ 6. to go for the gold

_____ 7. the odds

_____ 8. to be out in left field

a. to give up

b. to be crazy

c. the likelihood of success

d. to attack unfairly

e. to believe without question

f. to work well with others

g. to be on his side

h. to do something completely

C. Read the following list of additional sports expressions. Find out their meanings by asking English speakers or by using a dictionary. Then write a paragraph using as many of the expressions as you can. You may want to do this activity with a partner or in a small group.

1. to be on the ball _____

_____

2. to be par for the course_____

_____

3. to be in the ball park _____

_____

4. to hit a home run _____

_____

5. to be saved by the bell _____

_____

6. to have three strikes against you _____

_____

7. to play hard ball _____

_____

8. to slam dunk _____

_____

9. to bat a thousand_____

_____

10. to cover all the bases _____

_____

Now write your own paragraph.

_____

_____

_____

_____

_____

_____

_____

_____

_____

_____

D. What other sports expressions can you think of in English? Do you have any in your language? Write them on the lines below and explain them to your classmates.

_____

_____

_____

_____

_____

_____

_____

_____

_____

_____

JUST FOR FUN

WORD SEARCH

Find the names of twenty-four popular sports and circle them. The words may be horizontal, vertical, or diagonal. One word has been found for you. Then check your answers in the Answer Key on page 213.

gymnastics	ice skating	judo
horseracing	baseball	football
raquetball	soccer	wrestling
hockey	karate	golf
skiing	diving	archery
tennis	fishing	lacrosse
volleyball	bicycling	swimming
track	crew	basketball

```
G P D W X I S L A M L A C R O S S E B D E F G Q T U
O Y O E Y I P A G N X F T E R A C E G B D O G H I V
L V M G N J S F K T P S T F A M P Z Q O S O C S E W
F B C N E F J L T R V P M S O C C E R E R T A Z F Z
D E E C A B F A G A J I H A N K L M A O S B R P Q T
A T Y Z X S B W G C F V E I T U D C Q K L A H J I S
B D C A U V T Y W K X M N L P O Q Z U Z R L Q T S R
W I N M G P Q I F R O H S I T I U V E W J L W K L P
R A L Z M X N X C Q P R O N F G B H T E K C J I D Q
E W Y D E X F F I S H I N G A Z S B B C T U P V F N
S R X S Y G Z H I Q S A U T J W K V A L M E N O O D
T A D V X A M E R D W C R A A R A N L A Z Y T R B I
L S K I I N G I N S I B E C E V O L L E Y B A L L M
I K U W V D N E D O M I T T H L P Q R S G O O B S G
N B B C Y I E P S I M B O F T E Z Q R L S L A N N H
G L K F G I N I N N I S O M O B R C R W L M A I I L
D C A J H K L G O O N Y T A B C O Y E A T G L Y K K
H O R S E R A C I N G Z H E X Y C R B L E C D R I J
M J A P O S V U L T O R E D E O R T I U Y C D E E F
O E T Q R W U T W I L L I T V B E U I C C J U D O G
I C E S K A T I N G I S O B P K W K I B T I F Y I E
F P X Y Z A Z E B R A T T R S O Z B O S J A O J A A
H R I E B O B O Y S I J S A T I T H O C K E Y T I B
Q G C E N O P O P I S R B E G A D E C F B E Y O N C
S T B A S E B A L L O O B O T L A D F U G E T I N D
```

1. Historically, sports were "games" that we "played." Now, sports are big business in the United States, and professional athletes are highly paid celebrities. Is this true in your country? Is it true of all sports? Think of several sports for which it is not true.

2. New York humorist and journalist Irwin S. Cobb said in 1912: "As I understand it, sport is hard work for which you do not get paid." How has the idea of sports changed since 1912?

3. Joan Benoit Samuelson, an olympic gold medal winner, states: "Winning is neither everything nor the only thing; it is one of many things." This statement shows she understands the importance of keeping winning in perspective. How important do you think winning is in sports and in life?

4. There is a lot more to sports than the physical aspect of a game. The mental component is also extremely important. It includes concentration and self-confidence. In what ways does the psychology of sports affect the players and the outcome of a game?

5. Write a caption for the following cartoon.

Drawing by Chas. Addams; © 1940, 1968 The New Yorker Magazine, Inc.

READER'S JOURNAL

Write for ten to twenty minutes in your Reader's Journal about an aspect of sports. You might want to write about competition, a sports hero, traditional sports in your country, or any other aspect of sports that interests you.

READER'S JOURNAL

Date: _____

UNIVERSAL MYSTERIES

FYi

Unit•3

Selections

We use the word *mystery* to describe things we do not or cannot comprehend. Often we become very curious about these things and want to understand more about them. The world is full of mysteries. In this unit, you will read about several mysteries that scientists are trying to solve.

Think about and then discuss the following questions.

1. Do you ever find yourself wondering about the mysteries of the universe? Make a list of some of the most mysterious things you can think of.

_____

_____

_____

2. Some places on Earth are very mysterious. Can you think of some of these places? Discuss what you know or have heard about them.

_____

_____

_____

3. Researchers from many different branches of science are trying to solve the world's mysteries. But there are still many things they cannot explain. Do you think that advances in technology will help solve them? If so, what types of technologies will help us solve these unexplained mysteries?

_____

_____

_____

SELECTION 1

Ancient people were able to create many amazing things that we are not able to understand. In the following article, **The Mystery Statues of Easter Island**, you will read about mysterious statues on a small island in the Pacific Ocean.

BEFORE YOU READ

PREREADING DISCUSSION

1. Why do you think people are fascinated by mysteries from the past?

2. It is often said that we study the past to learn more about the future. What can we learn about the present and the future by studying the past?

FIRST READING   Read the article one time quickly and do the exercise that follows.

● ●

The Mystery Statues of Easter Island

D A N I E L   P O U E S I

1   EASTER ISLAND is a little island in Polynesia surrounded by one million empty square miles of Pacific Ocean. The closest inhabited land is tiny Pitcairn Island, which is about fourteen hundred miles away.

2   People have lived on Easter Island for hundreds of years. Long ago, the islanders farmed, using simple planting sticks and hoes. They made arrowheads and adzes[1] out of obsidian.[2] But these long-ago people also made huge and magnificent stone statues that have mystified scientists and everyone else for two centuries. Why did they do it? And how did they move the statues from the rock craters where they were carved to areas several miles away?

3   Of the 600 statues on the island, more than 150 are unfinished. They remain near and around the rim of the volcanic crater Rano Raraku. The tools used to carve them from the rock were found in the crater. It is as if the workers were called away suddenly and never came back.

---

1 adze A cutting tool with a thin arched blade used for shaping wood.
2 obsidian Very hard volcanic glass.

4   The statues have long earlobes, stomachs that stick out, jutting chins, and high foreheads. Their deep-set eyes make them seem old and wise. The largest, with its topknot,[3] stands as high as a seven-story building and weighs close to fifty tons. Imagine moving it, and you can understand why so many people were baffled.

5   Some people thought the ancient islanders might have had help from outer space. Others thought the islanders had magical powers. None of the explanations made sense until archeologists began to study the statues, the island, and the people living on the island today.

6   Archeologists study extinct cultures by examining abandoned house foundations, stone tools, and food remains and making guesses from these clues about what life in the past may have been like. They try to piece the jigsaw puzzle of past traditions together. Fact-finding for them is tough and tedious business. If they're lucky, they might find living descendants who know something about their people's roots and their ancestors, and how they did things in the past. Unfortunately, on Easter Island, very few of the natives knew about their past.

7   A terrible disaster occurred on Easter Island long before people arrived to study the island. In 1862, slavers transported a thousand natives bound hand and foot to Peru, South America. They were to work on plantations there. Of the hundred that were finally sent back, only fifteen reached the island. The survivors, however, brought smallpox with them and, as a result, more of their people died. In 1877, only 110 natives remained on the island.

8   In 1955, Thor Heyerdahl, a Norwegian expert on the history of people in the South Seas, arrived with a team of archeologists. Heyerdahl and the members of the expedition discovered things about the ancient people of Easter Island that no one had known before. But the experts still couldn't figure out how the statues had been raised.

9   One day Thor Heyerdahl offered the mayor of Easter Island, a man descended from one of the island's oldest families, one hundred dollars if he would place a statue back on its altar. The mayor accepted the challenge.

---

3 topknot Ornament forming a headdress.

10   The mayor organized men to gather stones and use poles. The poles were pushed under the statue's buried face. Men leaned on them to raise the face enough so that the mayor could shove stones under it. After nine days of work, the statue lay on a pile of stones so high that the men working the poles had to hang from them by ropes. On the eighteenth day, the statue was slid onto its altar. The archeologists saw that the topknot could be rolled up the pile of stones to rest on the statue's head.

11   Thor Heyerdahl was willing to pay the mayor his one hundred dollars. And the mayor showed Heyerdahl that the statues were probably moved on sleds made of forked trees and pulled by many people. He had learned these things from his father and grandfather. Why had he never told this to any of the other scientists who visited the island? "No one ever asked me," he said.

12   Later, William Mulloy, a member of Heyerdahl's team of archeologists, stayed on the island to raise more of the statues. From his experiments, he estimated that it would take "30 men one year to carve a stone statue, 90 men two months to move it, and 90 men three months to erect it."

13   In spite of their silence, these statues do communicate to us about the ancient people of Easter Island. To have carved, transported, and erected the statues, these people must have worked hard and cooperated with each other. The statues show us that not only can we learn *about* ancient people—we can also learn *from* them.

● ●

HOW WELL DID YOU READ?

Read the following statements. If a statement is true, write *T* on the line. If it is false, write *F*.

_____ 1. Easter Island is part of a group of small islands.

_____ 2. People have been living on Easter Island for hundreds of years.

_____ 3. All the statues on the island are completed.

_____ 4. Scientists have been curious about the statues on Easter Island for a long time.

_____ 5. Most of the statues are of young children.

_____ 6. Most of the Easter Islanders know a lot about their past.

_____ 7. Many natives of Easter Island died of smallpox.

_____ 8. The mayor of Easter Island knew how to raise a statue and put it back in its place.

SECOND READING

Now read the article again more carefully before answering the following questions about paragraph organization.

UNDERSTANDING ORGANIZATION

PARAGRAPHS

Using the numbers of the paragraphs in the article, identify the one(s) that

1. describes what archaeologists are and what they do ¶_____

2. tells how the men were able to raise the statues ¶_____

3. asks the questions that the rest of the article will answer ¶_____

4. gives some old theories about how the statues were built ¶_____

5. tells how the statues were moved ¶_____

6. describes what the statues look like ¶_____

7. discusses the disaster that happened on Easter Island in the mid-1800s ¶_____

SCANNING FOR DETAILS

Find the answers to the following questions as quickly as possible by scanning the article for the details you need.

1. How many statues are there on the island? _____

2. How tall is the largest statue? _____

3. How many natives lived on the island in 1877? _____

4. Who is Thor Heyerdahl? _____

5. How many men would it take to carve a stone statue? _____

FIGURE IT OUT

VOCABULARY IN CONTEXT

As you have learned, it is not always necessary to know the exact meaning of every word you read. For example, in the sentence, "Long ago, the islanders farmed, using simple planting sticks and *hoes*" you do not need to know exactly what *hoe* means. It is enough to understand that a hoe is something farmers used. You can guess that it has something to do with planting and need not waste time looking it up in the dictionary.

A. **Without using your dictionary, write an approximate definition or a synonym for the highlighted words in the following sentences. Then compare your answers with those of your classmates.**

1. *Easter Island is a little island in Polynesia **surrounded** by one million empty square miles of Pacific Ocean.*

   _____

2. ***Archeologists** study extinct cultures by examining abandoned house foundations, stone tools, and food remains and making guesses from these clues about what life in the past may have been like.*

   _____

3. *If they're lucky, they might find living **descendants** who know something about their people's roots and their ancestors, and how they did things in the past.*

   _____

B. In the following sentences, the highlighted words are all verbs. A *verb* is a word or phrase that tells what something or someone does, is, or experiences.
Try to understand the general sense of each sentence and then guess the meaning of the verb.

1. *But these long-ago people also made huge and magnificent stone statues that have **mystified** scientists and everyone else for two centuries. Why did they do it? And how did they move the statues from the rock craters . . . ?*

   _____

2. *The largest [statue] stands as high as a seven-story building and weighs close to fifty tons. Imagine moving it, and you can understand why so many people were **baffled.***

   _____

(continued on the next page)

The length of the Great Wall of China was nearly 3,000 miles when it was built.

3. The tools used to **carve** them from the rock were found in the crater.

_____

4. In 1862, slavers **transported** a thousand natives bound hand and foot to Peru, South America.

_____

5. The mayor organized men to gather stones and use poles. The poles were pushed under the statue's buried face. Men leaned on them to raise the face enough so that the mayor could **shove** stones under it.

_____

6. On the eighteenth day, the statue was **slid** onto its altar.

_____

7. To have carved, transported, and **erected** the statues, these people must have worked hard and **cooperated** with each other.

_____

_____

8. Heyerdahl and the members of the expedition discovered things about the ancient people of Easter Island that no one had known before. But the experts still couldn't **figure out** how the statues had been raised.

_____

9. From his experiments, he **estimated** that it would take "30 men one year to carve a statue, 90 men two months to move it, and 90 men three months to erect it."

_____

FYI

The Great Pyramid in Giza, Egypt, contains more than 2 million stones that average 2.3 metric tons each in weight.

SELECTION 2

There is a place in Peru that also has its share of mysteries. Like the statues on Easter Island, the lines on the Nazca plain in Peru have fascinated people for many years, but they still remain a mystery. Read all about it in the following article, **The Nazca Lines**.

BEFORE YOU READ

PREREADING ACTIVITY

Look at the photograph below. It was shot from an airplane flying above the Nazca plain in Peru.

What do you see? How big do you think the design is? Do you think it can be seen at ground level? How could it have been drawn? For what purpose(s)? And by whom, and when?

Try to answer the above questions. Then share your answers with your classmates.

_____

_____

_____

_____

_____

READING THE ARTICLE

Read the article quickly to see what people think of the Nazca lines.

● ●

The Nazca Lines

Suzanne Lord

1   The Nazca plain is in the southwestern section of Peru, in South America. It is only 38 miles inland from the Pacific Ocean.

2   When you stand on the ground there, the area looks harsh, dry, and rocky. Every so often, you might see small mounds of stones that look as if someone had deliberately put them there. But it's not mysterious-looking. The Nazca plain just looks like a barren area with little piles of rocks!

3   In an airplane, though, the Nazca plain looks quite different. Seen from above, you might see dozens of perfectly straight lines that look as if they had been drawn with a ruler. You might also see triangles, rectangles, or spirals. Or you might see, as though drawn on a giant blackboard, a monkey, a spider, a whale, a human hand, or a bird!

4   *Now* the Nazca plain is full of mysteries! Who made these lines and pictures? Why did they do it? Since they cannot be seen from the ground, whose attention were they supposed to have gotten?

5   Western civilization did not know about the Nazca lines until after the invention of the airplane. Their discovery was startling. Pilots, especially, looked at the rock-lined rectangles and realized that they looked for all the world like landing fields.

6   The thought of ancient, secret landing fields started wild theories about the lines. Some theories sound like science fiction stories.

7   One theory was that the "air-

fields" were built for "pilots" from the lost continent of Atlantis. When Atlantis sank, the airfields were of no further use. They were left as they were, to be found thousands of years later.

8   Another theory said that the "landing strips" were for UFOs. According to this theory, aliens landed on Earth in prehistoric times. They were friendly to our primitive ancestors. In fact, they may have taught early humans about the use of fire, or how to domesticate animals.

9   According to the theory, during their stay the aliens would be on their main ship most of the time. But sometimes they would shuttle to Earth's surface. The Nazca lines made it easy for the aliens to know where to land. The landing strip rectangles, the straight lines, and the animal pictures were for them to see—from the air.

10   These sensational theories brought the Nazca lines to the world's attention. From the 1970s on, people have been descending on Nazca to see the "ancient landing fields." (There really *is* an airfield in the area today—it is for planes bringing tourists!)

11   Scientists now have less sensational ideas. They know that humans lived in the area as far back as 12,000 years. But they feel that the lines, rectangles, and pictures were used for ritual rites or dances. The animal drawings may have represented different clans or tribes—the monkey clan, or the spider clan. The ancient peoples may have been trying to catch the attention of their gods.

12   One person had been studying and charting the Nazca lines long before they became famous. She is German mathematician Maria Reiche. The mathematical precision of the lines first attracted her attention in 1946.

13   Reiche had her own theory, based on her calculations. The Nazca lines are, she said, an astronomical chart. The animal figures may be clan figures for ancient gods. But the lines show movements of sun, stars, and planets over many years.

14   Scientists tried to test Reiche's theory by computer. They fed information about a section of lines into the computer. Then the computer matched this with positions of key stars as they would have appeared in the Peruvian sky thousands of years ago. The computer did not find a significant match.

15   Reiche said that the scientists did not have all of the data she had amassed. On the other hand, she was not willing to share her hard work with just anybody. Fortunately an astronomer from Chicago named Phyllis Pitluga gained Reiche's trust. Reiche shared her data with Pitluga, and the latter will publish Reiche's theory when it is ready.

16   In the meantime, the Nazca plain continues to be one of the Earth's most mysterious places. And the Nazca lines continue to raise more questions than they may ever answer.

Circle the letter of the phrase that best completes the sentence.

1. The Nazca plain looks mysterious _____.

   a. from all angles
   b. only from the ground
   c. from the air
   d. *(none of the above)*

2. The designs on the Nazca plain look like _____.

   a. geometric shapes
   b. animals
   c. perfectly straight lines
   d. *(all of the above)*

3. After the Nazca lines were discovered, _____.

   a. people were afraid to visit them
   b. many wild theories developed
   c. pilots began using them to help their landing
   d. scientists refused to pay any attention to them

4. Maria Reiche was interested in the _____ of the lines.

   a. mathematical precision
   b. unusual shapes and designs
   c. religious significance
   d. tourist appeal

5. Scientists believe the ancient people used the lines and drawings
   _____.

   a. for rituals
   b. to represent different clans and tribes
   c. to attract the attention of their gods
   d. *(all of the above)*

**MAKING
INFERENCES**

An **inference** is a conclusion that we make based on information that
we have. It is an educated guess. Good readers are constantly making
inferences based on information suggested in a reading passage.

**Read the following list of statements. If you think a statement is an
inference that can be drawn from information in the article, put a
check mark (✔) on the line.**

_____ 1. Tourists are interested in seeing the Nazca lines.

_____ 2. Computer tests proved Reiche's theory to be true.

_____ 3. Reiche trusted very few people with her work.

_____ 4. Ancient people lived in clans and tribes.

_____ 5. The Nazca lines were once landing strips for UFOs.

_____ 6. Ancient people had some form of religion.

THEORIES

The article mentions several theories that arose after the Nazca lines were discovered. The author refers to two of them as "wild" and "sensational" and others as scientific. By calling these theories wild and sensational, the author is contrasting them with the scientific ones:
— Wild and sensational theories are those not based on the prevalent views of mankind's history on Earth.
— Scientific theories rely on the traditional frameworks of interpretation.

List and describe the two theories that sound like science fiction stories and the two theories that sound more realistic.

A. Sensational Theories

1. _____

_____

2. _____

_____

B. Scientific Theories

1. _____

_____

2. _____

_____

Reading is an interactive process. The more you put into the reading process, the more you will get out of it. In other words, it is better to be an active reader than a passive reader because you will become more involved in what you are reading. One way to do this is to make predictions about what you are going to read. Titles, subtitles, headings, pictures, and charts can help you make predictions.

Before you read this article, look at the title, subtitles, and picture. Discuss them with your classmates, and predict what you think the article will be about. Write your prediction on the lines provided. After you read the article, check to see how close your prediction came.

_____

_____

_____

READING THE ARTICLE

Read the first three paragraphs of the article and answer the questions that follow before you continue with the rest of the article.

1. Why do you think the author uses the present tense to tell this story?

2. At what point did you realize that the man was going to die?

3. When do you think this story took place?

Frozen in Time

S A N D Y   F R I T Z

1   It's bitterly cold. The wind whips across the snowy mountains of Austria. A 25-year-old mountain climber stops to rest a moment on an icy slope. To warm up, he stomps his feet and blows on his numb fingers. After eating some berries, he slings his backpack over his shoulder and starts climbing again.

2   He picks his way over the rocks and ice—not knowing that he's almost at the end of his journey. At 10,500 feet up the mountainside, something happens.

3   The climber dies hunched over on his knees. Harsh winds quickly dry him out. Then his mummified body is covered with a blanket of snow. Slowly, the snow turns into ice, and he is forgotten.

4   More than 5,000 years pass. Then, last September, shocked hikers spotted the blackened body of the climber. (The cold gave his skin "freezer burn.") He was lying face down on a rocky shelf. The police were called in. They scrambled up to the two-mile-high location and picked up the frozen body.

Message from a Lost World

5   When medical examiners closely inspected his skin, they realized the man was from the distant past. They decided this was a job for Dr. Konrad Spindler. He is an expert on people who lived thousands of years ago.

6   "It took me about one second to realize how old he was," Dr. Spindler told CONTACT. "There was an ax found alongside the body that convinced me this was a man from the early metal age."

7   How did they know that the man really died around 3,000 B.C.? To find out, scientists carbon-dated his body. All living things contain the chemical carbon-14. When a plant or animal dies, it no longer absorbs carbon. And the carbon-14 already there slowly breaks down. So scientists could tell how old the body is by using a special instrument to measure how much carbon-14 is left. (The older it is, the less carbon it will have.)

8   The body—well preserved by the ice—may be the oldest ever found in Europe. "It may be one of the most important finds in the century!" Dr. Spindler exclaims. "We know very little about prehistoric people. All we have are some bones, tools, and a few remains of houses." But the body will now allow scientists to get a better idea of what life was like 5,000 years ago.

Otze the Iceman

9   Scientists nicknamed the iceman "Otze" (URT-sey), for the Otztaler region where he was found. "Otze had dark, almost black hair," says Dr. Spindler, adding that his long hair fell out when he was mummified by the cold, dry wind. (Researchers discovered hair lying around the body.) Another big surprise: Otze has blue tatoos—made from vegetable inks—on his back, his knees, and his ankles! So far, no one knows if the line and crosses tattooed on his body mean anything. Scientists also found a stone bead necklace. They think he may have worn it as a "good luck" charm.

10   Otze's clothes, little of which remain, are interesting too. "We know he wore a fur-lined leather coat," says Dr. Spindler. He also wore a cape of tightly woven reeds to block wind and snow. Otze's leather trousers and shoes were stuffed with hay to help keep him warm.

11   Researchers found some grains, dried fruit, animal bones, and other belongings near the body. "He carried a flint knife with a wooden handle, arrows, a flint for starting fires, a small leather pouch, and a birch-bark backpack."

12   Scientists were astonished when they discovered his bow. Otze himself only stood about five feet, three inches tall. But his bow was almost five feet, 10 inches long! Like the bow, the flint-tipped arrows were extremely large, almost three feet long.

13   "The bow, as well as the arrows, were not yet ready for use," says Dr. Spindler. Since the weapons weren't ready to fire, scientists think Otze must not have felt he was in danger.

14   "Otze was obviously an experienced mountain climber," observes Dr. Spindler. "His clothes and belongings showed that he was well-prepared for living days, even weeks, on the mountains. Death must have taken him by surprise."

Testing the Ice

15   Today, Otze is kept in a special room at the University of Innsbruck. To keep him preserved, the room temperature remains around 21 degrees F. This summer, lots of tests will be done on Otze. "We'll have about 100 scientists working on different projects," says Dr. Spindler.

16   "Specialists in medicine, archeology, and biology will all help with the tests." What will they be looking for? Scientists will study his tools and clothing to find out how they were made. The body itself will be tested to see if Otze suffered from any viruses

or diseases, such as arthritis. Scientists will even figure out what Otze ate by looking inside his stomach and at his teeth. (His teeth are worn down—typical of a time when people ate lots of meat and coarse grains.)

17   Already, a team of experts is using high-tech X-rays to peer inside the body. "We want to test as much as possible without cutting the body itself," says Dr. Spindler. These 3-D images may also help scientists reconstruct the way he actually looked.

18   Dr. Spindler will peer into Otze's DNA to discover any differences between him and modern humans. (DNA is found in cells and determines the body's characteristics.) He also plans to compare Otze's samples to DNA samples of people now living in the Austrian mountains to see if they are related.

19   "We will also try to find out what the cause of death was," says Dr. Spindler. "I think he lost his way and died of cold in a blizzard."

20   Why was Otze in the mountains in the first place? Was he there to mine copper, to hunt, or trade goods with a settlement on the other side? No one knows. And some mysteries about his life—and his death—may never be solved.

● ●

UNDERSTANDING THE ARTICLE

"Frozen in Time" is divided into four parts. The purpose of the first part is to introduce the subject and get readers curious and excited about the topic. Look at the other three parts. Each one has a heading suggesting what the section will be about. In the space provided, write the three headings and a summary of the main ideas of each section.

Part 2 Subtitle _____

Part 2 Summary _____

_____

Part 3 Subtitle _____

_____

Part 3 Summary _____

_____

(continued on the next page)

Part 4 Subtitle _____

Part 4 Summary _____

_____

MAKING INFERENCES

Read the following list of statements. If you think a statement is true because the article states it directly or you can infer it, write *T* on the line. If you think it is false, write *F*. If you think that no conclusion can be drawn from information in the article, write *N*.

_____ 1. The tattoos on Otze's body had religious significance.

_____ 2. Some ancient people wore stone necklaces for good luck.

_____ 3. Otze knew how to dress to keep warm in the mountains.

_____ 4. Otze knew he was about to die.

_____ 5. Otze's diet included meat and grains.

_____ 6. Otze came to the mountain to mine copper.

_____ 7. People 5,000 years ago knew how to use metal.

_____ 8. Freezing a body in ice can preserve it for thousands of years.

_____ 9. Scientists can learn a lot by comparing Otze to modern humans.

_____ 10. Otze was related to the people living in the Austrian mountains today.

_____ 11. Otze was not a skilled mountain climber.

APPLICATION OF INFORMATION

Write a physical description of Otze on the day he died. In your paragraph, include what he looked like as well as what he was wearing and what he had with him.

_____

_____

_____

HOW WELL DID YOU READ?

Answer the following questions.

1. The article discusses several ways scientists can find out information about the past. What kinds of scientists worked on the team?

2. How did scientists determine when Otze died? Explain the process.

3. How did scientists find out information about Otze's diet?

4. How can they reconstruct the way he actually looked?

5. How can they discover differences between Otze and modern man?

BUILDING VOCABULARY SKILLS

PREFIXES

You have already studied the prefixes meaning *no* or *not*. In this article, several more prefixes are used. Read the following sentences, paying attention to the highlighted words.

*We know very little about **prehistoric** people.*

*These 3-D images may also help scientists **reconstruct** the way he actually looked.*

The prefix *pre-* means *first* or *before*, so *prehistoric* means *before history*. The prefix *re-* means *again* or *back*. What do you think the word *reconstruct* means?

A. Look at the following list of words. Notice how the meaning changes when you add the prefix *pre-* or *re-*. Write the meaning of each new word on the line provided.

1. arrange: rearrange_____

　　　　　　　prearrange _____

2. view: review _____

　　　　　　preview _____

3. pay: repay_____

　　　　　prepay_____

4. reading: rereading_____

　　　　　　　prereading_____

5. test: retest _____

　　　　　pretest _____

(continued on the next page)

Some other common prefixes in English and their meanings include

bi- meaning *two*   **multi-** meaning *many*
tri- meaning *three*   **trans-** meaning *across*
co- meaning *together*   **inter-** meaning *between*
mis- meaning *wrong*   **il-** meaning *bad*
non- meaning *no*

B. Listed below are some examples of these prefixes in use. Try to figure out the meaning of each word and write a definition on the line provided.

1. bilingual _____

2. cooperate _____

3. illogical _____

4. interstate _____

5. misunderstand _____

6. triangle _____

7. multipurpose _____

8. transatlantic _____

9. interactive _____

10. tricycle _____

11. coauthor _____

12. miscommunicate _____

13. multilingual _____

14. illegal _____

15. nonsense _____

C. Use each of the following words in a sentence.

1. intercontinental

_____

_____

2. co-author

_____

_____

3. multimedia

_____

_____

4. transport

_____

_____

5. nonsense

_____

_____

6. misinterpret

_____

_____

7. biannual

_____

_____

In a library in Connecticut, there is a very mysterious book written over eight hundred years ago. No one can figure out who wrote it or what it says because it was written in a secret code. The most mysterious thing about this book is its pictures, which show groups of stars and parts of our bodies that are not visible to the human eye. Neither the telescope nor the microscope had been invented when the book was written.[1]

[1] Florence Munat, _FACTS-ination_; Scholastic Book Services, 1976, 41.

NASA Listens for Space Aliens describes the plans for a ten-year project to listen for radio waves sent from alien civilizations. It began in the fall of 1992. Unfortunately, the project cost too much money ($1 million a month), and it was canceled after only one year.

BEFORE YOU READ

PREREADING ACTIVITY

Have you ever looked up at the stars and wondered about life on other planets? Write a brief paragraph about what life outside the planet Earth might be like. Use the words below to write your paragraph. You can use the words in any order, but try to use every word. Before you write, discuss the meaning of any unfamiliar word with your teacher and classmates.

UFO • signals • intelligent • outer space • life • future
• amazing • extraterrestrial • universe • alone • contact
• technology • human

_____

_____

_____

_____

_____

_____

_____

_____

_____

_____

_____

READING THE ARTICLE

Read the article one time quickly for main ideas.

NASA Listens for Space Aliens

A N D R E W   R A G A N

You're listening to the Top 40 Countdown on your boom box when a weird voice breaks in. "Attention Earthlings!" it says. "This is Bandor from the planet Pyron in the Constellation Zebo. We have received a transmission from you humans. You are not alone in the universe...."

1   NASA, the U.S. space agency, believes there's a good chance we're not alone in the universe. Last fall, NASA began a new project called the High Resolution Microwave Survey (HRMS). Its aim: to find evidence of life in one of the billions of galaxies in the universe.

2   The search for intelligent life on other planets isn't new. It began almost 100 years ago. That's when scientists built a huge transmitter to beam radio waves into space. Scientists thought smart beings on other planets might pick up the signals.

3   Scientists also have beamed a message about humans and our solar system to a nearby constellation. But because the constellation is 25,000 light years away, a return message wouldn't reach Earth for 50,000 years! So don't wait up for an answer.

4   So far, no ETs (extraterrestrial

beings) that we know of have returned our "calls." But according to Dr. Jill Tarter, an HRMS scientist, we haven't exactly had our ears wide open. "Now, however," says Dr. Tarter, "we've built the tools we need to listen well."

5   Last October, Dr. Tarter switched on the largest radio receiver in the world. It's an enormous metal bowl stretching 1,000 feet across a canyon in the jungles of Puerto Rico.

6   Meanwhile, another NASA scientist flipped on a huge radio antenna in California's Mojave Desert. NASA hopes these big dishes—and others around the world—will pick up radio signals from new worlds.

7   Dr. Frank Drake has been searching for life in outer space for years. He explains the HRMS project this way: To listen to your radio, you move the tuner on the dial until the channels come in loud and clear. Now imagine radio receivers that scan our galaxy "listening" to 14 million channels every second. That's what NASA's radio telescopes in Puerto Rico and California are doing.

8   But that's not all. Powerful computers hooked to the telescopes sift through every signal. The computers try to match the signals to ones that scientists already recognize, such as human-made signals. If they can't,

Drake and Tarter check on them. "It could prove there is radio technology elsewhere in the universe," says Dr. Tarter. "And that would mean we're not alone."

9   "Whenever I look up at the stars," Dr. Tarter adds, "it seems ridiculous to think we are alone." After all, she reasons, there are billions of galaxies like our own. And in each of those galaxies are hundreds of billions of stars like our sun. Since each sun might also have planets, it's very likely that some of those planets support life as Earth does. And, she believes, some of that life could be intelligent.

10   That leads right to the next big question: If there are smart ETs out there, are they trying to reach us? There's no way to know for sure. But according to Dr. Tarter, it might not matter. "If they have the technology, their signals may reach us by accident, just as our TV signals may reach them." Dr. Drake is also confident. "I fully expect to find signals from an extraterrestrial before the year 2000," he says.

11   Not all scientists are that certain of discovering life in other galaxies. But who knows? If Dr. Drake is correct, the year 2000 just might bring us a group of new space neighbors!

● ●

HOW WELL DID YOU READ?

Underline the word or phrase that makes the sentence true according to the article.

1. NASA (believes / does not believe) that we are alone in the universe.

2. (All / Not all) scientists are certain of discovering life on other galaxies.

3. Scientists (have beamed / will beam) a message about humans and our solar system to a nearby constellation.

4. If we receive an answer from that constellation, it will take (5,000 / 50,000) years to reach us.

5. Powerful computers (try to / can always) match incoming signals to the ones scientists already recognize.

USING ABBREVIATIONS

We often use abbreviations or acronyms to shorten a long word or group of words. Abbreviations are very common in technical and scientific writing.

A. Explain what each of the following abbreviations from this unit means.

1. ET _____

2. NASA _____

3. HRMS _____

4. UFO _____

5. 3-D _____

6. DNA _____

7. B.C. _____

B. A common English abbreviation is highlighted in each of the following sentences. Try to find out what each one stands for. Use clues from the context of the sentences.

1. Foreign students need to take the *TOEFL* in order to be admitted to an American university.

TOEFL _____

_____

2. Most universities in the United States require a certain score on the *SAT* for admittance.

SAT _____

(continued on the next page)

3. When a federal law is broken, the *FBI* may be called in to help investigate the case.

   FBI _____

4. At the bottom of the invitation, the host wrote *BYO*.

   BYO _____

5. Many of the world's most successful businessmen have an *MBA* from a good university.

   MBA _____

6. It is the dream of many basketball players to play on an *NBA* team.

   NBA _____

7. An important aspect of marketing any product is *PR*.

   PR _____

8. It usually takes at least five or six years of hard work to get a *Ph.D.* in history, economics, or anthropology.

   Ph.D. _____

9. I'm not sure exactly what time the ship will dock, but the *ETA* is 5:00 P.M.

   ETA _____

10. The *CEO* of a company has a lot of decision-making power.

    CEO _____

11. The note said, "*FYI*, the meeting has been canceled. It is rescheduled for tomorrow at noon."

    FYI _____

12. Please finish this important report *ASAP*.

    ASAP _____

C. **What other abbreviations have you heard English speakers use? Find three or four abbreviations and bring them to class. Exchange your list with a classmate and find out what each one means.**

Abbreviation	Meaning
_____	_____
_____	_____
_____	_____
_____	_____

TALK IT OVER

DISCUSSION
QUESTIONS

1. Do you believe there is life on other planets? Have you or anyone you know ever seen a UFO?

2. In the introduction to this reading you learned that this project was canceled because it cost too much money. Do you think that this was a wise decision? Why? How do you feel about governments spending money on this type of investigation?

3. What other space projects do you know about? Do you think they should be continued or canceled? Why?

Answer each of the following questions in the spaces provided. Then, follow the directions to solve the puzzle. Finally, check your answers in the Answer Key on page 213.

1. When you look at the Nazca plains from above, you might see some perfectly straight _____.

   ___ ___ ___ ⬭ ___

2. What is Mr. Heyerdahl's first name?

   ⬭ ___ ___ ___

3. What is the abbreviation for the U.S. space agency?

   ___ ___ ⬭ ___

4. What was the 5,000-year-old man found in?

   ⬭ ___ ___

5. What is a group of stars?

   ___ ___ ___ ___ ___ ⬭

6. There are many _____ about the Easter Island statues.

   ___ ___ ___ ___ ⬭ ___ ___ ___

7. What do scientists beam to other constellations?

   ⬭ ___ ___ ___ ___ ___ ___ ___

8. Where is Easter Island located?

   ___ ___ ___ ___ ___ ⬭ ___ ___ ___

9. What are people from the planet Earth known as?

   ⬭ ___ ___ ___ ___ ___ ___ ___ ___

You will notice that one letter for each answer is circled. Write the nine circled letters below. Then unscramble them to find a word about this unit.

____ ____ ____ ____ ____ ____ ____ ____ ____

10. _____

ORAL REPORTS

1. This unit has included mention of only a few of the many mysteries in our world. There are dozens more. Look over the list that follows and choose one that interests you. Then find out some interesting information about it, and prepare a short oral presentation for your class.

Stonehenge (England)	Abominable Snowman (Asia)
Angkor Wat (Cambodia)	The Pyramids (Egypt)
Loch Ness Monster (Scotland)	Bermuda Triangle (Atlantic Ocean)

2. Find a magazine or newspaper article that reports a story about a recent mysterious event such as a UFO sighting. Bring the article to class and share it with your classmates.

POSTREADING DISCUSSION QUESTIONS

1. It has been said, "The nature of reality remains an *inexplicable* mystery." What does "inexplicable" mean? What does the quote mean? How does it relate to the articles you have read and to your own research?

2. Albert Einstein once said, "He who finds a thought that lets us even a little deeper into the eternal mystery of nature has been granted great grace." What do you think Einstein means by, "eternal mystery of nature?" Do you agree or disagree with what Einstein said? What are your reasons?

READER'S JOURNAL

Write for ten to twenty minutes in your Reader's Journal about your reactions to the ideas in this unit. You may want to describe other mysteries you know about or write about your own experiences with the mysteries of the universe.

READER'S JOURNAL

Date: _____

OUR **F**RAGILE **P**LANET

FYi

Unit·4

Selections

All over the world people are becoming increasingly conscious of their responsibility for the health of our planet. Environmental issues are getting more attention than ever before. For example, many countries are introducing recycling programs for glass, aluminum, and paper. Stricter laws are being passed to decrease pollution. In fact, concerned people everywhere are joining together to celebrate "Earth Day" on April 22 each year.

Think about and then discuss the following questions.

1. Make a list of some things that are threatening our environment. In what ways have people helped and hurt the environment?

_____

_____

_____

2. What steps are being taken by individuals, organizations, and countries to correct some of the problems facing our planet?

_____

_____

_____

3. Do you consider yourself to be an environmentally conscious person? What things do you personally do to help protect our environment?

_____

_____

_____

In the following interview, **One Family with the Earth**, a Native American medicine man discusses the special relationship of his people with the land.

BEFORE YOU READ

PREREADING DISCUSSION

1. What do you think is meant by the title, "One Family with the Earth"?

2. Read Chief Seattle's quote at the beginning of the interview and discuss it with your classmates. Why do you suppose he calls the flowers "our sisters" and the deer, horse, and eagle "our brothers"?

Complete Chief Seattle's quote with your own words and ideas. Then compare them with those of your classmates.

We are part of the earth and it is part of us. The _____ are

our sisters; the _____, _____, _____, these

are our brothers. The _____, the _____ in the

_____, the _____ of the _____, and

_____ —all belong to the same family.

● ● ● ● ● ● ● ● ● ● ● ● ● ● ● ● ● ● ● ●

One Family with the Earth

We are part of the earth and it is part of us. The perfumed flowers are our sisters; the deer, the horse, the great eagle, these are our brothers. The rocky crests, the flowers in the meadows, the body heat of the pony, and man—all belong to the same family.
Chief Seattle of the Suquamish, 1854

Native people think about the preservation of the earth, plants, and animals in a special way. Medicine Story (Manitonquat), a storyteller and a keeper of the lore of the Wampanoag Nation of Massachusetts and ceremonial medicine man of the Assonet band, talks with people across the country in his work as a writer and educator. He says that native people around the world share the attitude that the earth is spiritually alive and that people may live with it but do not own it.

How do native people view the earth?

1   As a native, I have been taught that we must be the caretakers of the earth. We call the earth our mother because taking care of it is a primary responsibility, like caring for our parents and our children. Our people are taught to act and walk lightly upon this earth in a sacred manner, making every step upon the Earth Mother as a prayer so that seven generations yet to come may follow our paths in safety.

Did native people of America practice any conservation measures before other settlers came?

2   Native people were environmentally conscious because they lived close to the environment. Others don't realize how much care they took in the woods. In everything they did, they were conscious of the fact that if you disturb something, it will have ramifications through the whole web of life. So they were very careful about disturbing anything.

3   Human beings are very intelligent and take good care of themselves. But what happened in civilization is that human beings' intelligence went off in other directions and developed tech-

nology, arts, and such things to the point where they began to be removed from their natural environment. When you build a city around you, the younger generations begin to think that milk comes from a carton and not from an animal.

How did Native Americans view the arrival of European settlers?

4   When Europeans first came, the Native Americans welcomed them and thought they would act like human beings in the natives' understanding of how human beings are supposed to relate to the earth. But the Europeans came here with conquest in mind. They took land they could take, bought what they could buy, and stole and fought for the rest. Suddenly we discovered that they thought we were subjects of their kings and that we had given them this land forever. Nobody owns land. You can use it, have your animals on it, hunt, and so forth, but the land is here forever. We are part of it.

What needs to be done for the earth?

5   We need to think about a whole new set of values to give to our kids. A lot of native people like myself go to schools whenever we get a chance. We take the kids out into the woods and say, "Here, these are your relatives. Sit with this tree. Talk to this tree. Listen to this tree. Hug this tree. This is your friend."

6   The earth and our fellow creatures are more valuable than all the fancy things we have. It should horrify all human beings that we are losing whole species of animals and birds. There are no free-flying California condors left in California, and several hundred beluga whales in the St. Lawrence River are dying of cancer from industrial wastes.

What do we need to do to be friends with the earth?

7   One thing people can do is to get closer to the earth. If you go camping or on a picnic, take the time to look at what's around and talk about the plants, birds, and whatever comes by.

8   When I was a kid, my grandfather took me out. We had names for all the animals, and he told me about the plants. He told me to talk to them and to listen to them. He said there were stones that had spirits. You could feel the spirit and know that it had been there for a long time and had seen a lot of things; you could get a lot of knowledge from that stone.

What does it mean to be friends with the earth?

9   When you're somebody's friend, you don't let anybody hurt him, you stick up for him. It makes you feel good to be with him.

10   Everything in the universe is important; everything has its purpose and its reason. We are here as part of the earth. It was put here for more than just our pleasure. It must support many things.

11   Often I say to children that if you are the elder brother or sister, you have to speak for the little baby who cannot talk. You speak for the grass because it's not able to talk. If you were a blade of grass, what would you say? If you were a little squirrel, what would you say? If you were the Mother Earth herself, what would you say about what's happening to you?

> *You must remember that [the land] is sacred, and you must teach your children that it is sacred.*
> Chief Seattle's prophesy, 1854

**UNDERSTANDING
MAIN IDEAS**

INTERPRETING THE
ARTICLE

**Which of the following statements would Manitonquat agree with?
Put a check in front of those statements. Defend your answer with
evidence from the text—the first one is done for you.**

✔ 1. Taking care of the earth should be one of man's fundamental
responsibilities.

   Manitonquat says that "taking care of it [the earth] is a primary

   responsibility, like caring for our parents and our children." (¶ 1)

____ 2. Acts committed against the environment are done in isolation.

_____

____ 3. Land should belong to whoever is willing to fight the hardest
for it or pay the most money for it.

_____

____ 4. We should treasure the earth and all living plants and animals
more than expensive things we can buy.

_____

____ 5. We don't need to worry too much about endangered species.
The earth will recover naturally on its own.

_____

____ 6. It is only possible to communicate with and learn from living
creatures.

_____

____ 7. Only some things in the world are important. We can ignore
other things.

_____

____ 8. The European settlers' view of man's relationship with the earth
surprised the Native Americans.

_____

FIGURE IT OUT

VOCABULARY IN
CONTEXT

Without using your dictionary, write an approximate definition or a synonym for the highlighted words in the following sentences. Then explain how the context helped you arrive at your answer.

1. *Native people think about the **preservation** of the earth, plants, and animals in a special way.*

   to preserve = to protect, to take care of

   CLUE: Earth, plants, and animals "all belong to the same family."

   Members of the same family protect, take care of one another.

2. *As a native, I have been taught that we must be the **caretakers** of the earth.*

   _____

   CLUE: _____

3. *Our people are taught to act and walk lightly upon this earth in a **sacred** manner, making every step upon the Earth Mother as a prayer. . . .*

   _____

   CLUE: _____

4. *In everything they did, they were conscious of the fact that if you disturb something, it will have **ramifications** through the whole web of life.*

   _____

   CLUE: _____

5. *But the Europeans came here with **conquest** in mind. They took what land they could take, bought what they could buy, and stole and fought for the rest.*

   _____

   CLUE: _____

6. *It should **horrify** all human beings that we are losing whole species of animals and birds.*

   _____

   CLUE: _____

(continued on the next page)

7. *There are no free-flying California* **condors** *left in California.*

_____

CLUE: _____

8. *When you're somebody's friend, you don't let anybody hurt him, you* **stick up** *for him.*

_____

CLUE: _____

TALK IT OVER

DISCUSSION
QUESTIONS

1. According to Manitonquat, native people everywhere feel that the earth is spiritually alive and that we may live with the earth, but we do not own it. Do you agree with this philosophy? Why or why not?

2. What does Manitonquat think happened when man began to be removed from the natural environment? How did man come to be removed from the environment?

3. How would you describe the Native Americans' relationship with the earth? What about their attitude toward the environment? In what ways is it similar to or different from the attitude in your country?

4. Manitonquat's grandfather told him it was possible to get a lot of knowledge from a stone. What did he mean by that?

APPLICATION OF INFORMATION

Think about the last three questions in the interview. How would you answer each one?

1. *What needs to be done for the earth?*

_____

_____

_____

2. *What do we need to do to be friends with the earth?*

_____

_____

_____

3. *What does it mean to be friends with the earth?*

_____

_____

_____

READING
FURTHER

The following passage expresses the thoughts of a holy woman of the Wintu Indians of California. As you read, think about the similarities between her beliefs and those of Manitonquat.

The White people never cared for land or deer or bear. When we Indians kill meat, we eat it all up. When we dig roots, we make little holes. When we burn grass for grasshoppers, we don't ruin things. We shake down acorns and pinenuts. We don't chop down the trees. We only use dead wood. But the White people plow up the ground, pull down the trees, kill everything. The tree says, "Don't. I am sore. Don't hurt me." But they chop it down and cut it up. The spirit of the land hates them. They blast out trees and stir it up to their depths. They saw up the trees. That hurts them. The Indians never hurt anything, but the White people destroy all. They blast rocks and scatter them on the ground. The rock says, "Don't. You are hurting me." But the White people pay no attention. When Indians use rocks, they take little round ones for their cooking. . . . How can the spirit of the earth like the White man? Everywhere the White man has touched it, it is sore.[1]

TALK IT OVER

DISCUSSION
QUESTIONS

1. In your own words, contrast the ways the Native Americans use the earth with the ways other people do.
2. What small changes can each of us make in our habits so the earth will not be so sore?

90 percent of all trash can be recycled.

[1]Dorothy Lee, *Freedom and Culture* (Englewood Cliffs: Prentice-Hall, 1959), 163ff.

Overpopulation and world hunger are two of the most serious problems human beings now face. The following article, **Too Many Mouths to Feed?**, discusses these problems and suggests some possible solutions.

1. What do you think are some of the biggest problems facing our planet today? Make a list of the five you think are the most serious. Put them in order of importance and compare your list with those of your classmates.

   a._____

   b._____

   c._____

   d._____

   e._____

2. In groups, discuss some possible solutions to these problems.

Now read the following article.

● ●

Too Many Mouths to Feed?

1   How many people can live on the face of the earth? No one knows the answer. It depends on how much food people can grow without destroying the environment.

2   More people now exist than ever before, and the population keeps growing. Every 15 seconds, about 100 babies are born. By the year 2000, experts say, as many as 6 *billion* people will live on this planet. Before the end of the next century, the earth may hold 10 billion people!

3   To feed everyone, farmers must grow more food. They are trying to do so. World food production has gradually risen over the years. In some parts of the world, however, the population is growing faster than the food supply. Some experts fear the world will not be able to produce enough food for a population that never stops increasing.

4   To grow more crops on the same amount of land, farmers use fertilizers and pesticides. Some plant new kinds of grains that produce more food. These things help—but they don't provide perfect solutions. The chemicals in fertilizers and pesticides can pollute water supplies. The new seeds developed by scientists may have reached the limit of what they can produce.

5   When hungry people can coax no more out of existing farmland, they search for more. Usually, the best land is already in use. People have to scratch new farms into steep hillsides or carve fields out of forests.

6   As people clear trees from hills and forests, they expose the soil. Then rain and floods may strip the topsoil from fields. Winds may blow it away. This process is called erosion. Each year erosion steals billions of tons of topsoil from farmers—soil they could have used to grow food.

7   Destruction of trees, erosion, and overgrazing by farm animals can turn fertile land into desert. And deserts can spread. The Sahara Desert in North Africa, for example, is moving southward. Its shifting sands are gradually smothering villages and fields.

8   To farmers water can be as important as the land. In recent years irrigation has made many dry areas bloom. Yet experts warn that some forms of irrigation can hurt the land in the long run. Sometimes irrigation water contains large quantities of dissolved salt. Over time the salt builds up in the soil and kills plants.

9   This harvest of problems demands solutions. But experts disagree about what should be done. Some believe birthrates must fall or the world will run out of food. "Without reducing the size of the human population," says Stanford University Professor Paul Ehrlich, "none of these problems is likely to be solved."

10   Other experts believe the earth can provide enough food for all. Pierre Crosson and Norman Rosenberg of Resources for the Future, a research group, say that world food production could grow much more slowly than the current rate, and there would still be enough food for ten billion people. Still, getting the food to those who need it is a problem. In some tropical countries, two-thirds of the world's people live on only one-fifth of the world's food.

11   Most hungry people live in developing countries—those without much modern industry. The people lack money to buy food and means to transport it. If nations with surplus food try to help, donations may not reach those who need them. Bad roads, politics, and warfare often block delivery.

12   Since no one can predict the future, no one knows how long the world's food supply will feed its people. Most experts favor a two-part attack on hunger: Bring food supplies up and birth rates down.

13   Better education for women in developing countries can help do both. Women do much of the farm work in these countries. Education will help them get the most out of agricultural assistance. They can also take advantage of family planning information.

14   Scientists can aid the war against hunger by developing crops that resist disease and by improving irrigation methods. People everywhere must learn how to grow food without harming the environment.

15   Population and hunger are global problems. No one nation can solve them. "We have created the fix in which society finds itself," says Ehrlich, "but we still have the opportunity and ability to pull ourselves out of it—if we act rapidly and with determination. Our species is capable of providing all its members with a satisfying, productive life in a healthy environment. No great scientific breakthroughs are required—just a collective determination to change our minds and our ways."

HOW WELL DID YOU READ?

Read the following statements. If a statement is true, write _T_ on the line. If it is false, write _F_.

_____ 1. Scientists know how many people the earth can support.

_____ 2. World food production has not risen over the years.

_____ 3. There are several ways to grow more food on the same amount of land.

_____ 4. Irrigation has both positive and negative effects on the land.

_____ 5. Erosion causes the earth to lose some of its valuable farm land.

_____ 6. All experts agree on the best way to solve the problems of food supply and population.

_____ 7. The earth's population is evenly distributed and the food supply is equally divided among all people.

_____ 8. Most hungry people live in developing countries.

_____ 9. Increasing food supplies and decreasing the birth rate are two ways to help solve the earth's hunger problem.

_____ 10. No single nation can be responsible for solving global problems of population and hunger.

IDENTIFYING MAIN IDEAS

Recognizing the main idea of a paragraph will help you understand the meaning of a paragraph as a whole. A particular sentence of a paragraph (often the first or last) can express the main idea. Sometimes, however, you need to draw a general conclusion based the information in the paragraph.

Circle the statement that best describes the main idea.

PARAGRAPH 2

a. One hundred babies are born every fifteen seconds.

b. Before the end of the next century, the earth may hold 10 billion people.

c. The world's population is rapidly increasing.

(continued on the next page)

PARAGRAPH 6

a. As people clear trees from hills and forests, they expose the soil.

b. Erosion is a serious problem because it strips away soil used for growing food.

c. Winds may blow soil away.

PARAGRAPH 10

a. Although the earth may be able to provide enough food for everyone, getting it to hungry people is a problem.

b. Two-thirds of the world's people live on one-fifth of the world's food.

c. Food production could slow down and there would still be enough food for everyone.

PARAGRAPH 13

a. Better education for women can help solve problems of food supply and overpopulation.

b. Women should learn about family planning.

c. Most farming is done by women.

PARAGRAPH 15

a. Great scientific breakthroughs are needed to solve the global problems facing us now.

b. Population and hunger are global problems that require collective action by all nations.

c. Man has created the global problems that are troubling our planet.

UNDERSTANDING THE ARTICLE

PROBLEMS AND SOLUTIONS

The article you have just read explores world problems and offers solutions. To understand the meaning of the article, you need to examine these problems and solutions and analyze their causes and effects.

1. What two main problems does the article discuss?

   a._____   b._____

2. What two primary solutions to these problems does the article suggest?

   a. _____

   b. _____

3. The author discusses ways to accomplish the solutions. What are some ways the food supply can be increased?

   a. _____

   b. _____

   c. _____

4. Some solutions may have negative effects on the environment. What are the negative effects of each of the following possible solutions?

   a. Irrigation: _____

   b. Cutting trees from hills and forests to make more farmland: _____

   _____

   c. Using fertilizers and pesticides: _____

   _____

FYI

The world's rain forests are being cut down at a rate of fifty acres per minute. (That is the size of about twenty-eight soccer fields.)

5. What two groups of people should be part of the solution? What can each group do?

   a. _____

   b. _____

6. The author also examines the causes and results of problems. According to the article, getting food to hungry people is a big problem. List three causes of this problem.

   a. _____

   b. _____

   c. _____

7. What is the result of overgrazing, erosion, and cutting trees?

   _____

8. How can education help save the environment?

   _____

The previous articles looked at the global problems of overpopulation and hunger. This article, **Our Endangered Wildlife**, investigates the effect that people have on the environment, especially on other animals and plants.

Before you read the article look at the introduction. What do you think the author means by "humans have become the most powerful living beings on earth. This power gives us a special responsibility." What kinds of responsibility do we have toward our earth?

Our Endangered Wildlife

Over many thousands of years, humans have become the most powerful living beings on earth. That power gives us a special responsibility. In this, the first of a series on the environment, WORLD explores the impact humans have on the earth and on other living things that share the earth.

1   Before this day ends, the last of some 45 kinds of plants and animals will die. A month from now, 1,400 more species will be gone. Within a year, the number of vanished species will total about 17,500. Scientists provide these estimates, which represent the most *hopeful* case. The actual numbers may prove to be much higher.

2   Among the vanishing species are African elephants. Ivory hunters kill the elephants illegally at the rate of about 200 a day. Farmers in overcrowded countries squeeze elephant herds into spaces too small to support them. Ten years ago $1\frac{1}{2}$ million elephants roamed the African countryside. Now perhaps 400,000 remain.

3   Loss of the elephant, nearly everyone agrees, would be tragic. Even worse, say scientists, would be the loss of smaller, often microscopic species. "It's the tiny species that really run the planet," says Dr. Thomas Lovejoy, a conservationist with the Smithsonian Institution in Washington, D.C. "Bacteria make digestion possible. Fungi give us penicillin and other medicines. Grass and other plants contribute oxygen. 'Squirmies' such as worms and termites are nature's recyclers."

4   Huge numbers of *unknown* plants and animals are also in danger. The earth, according to various estimates, supports between 5 million and *80 million* species. Of these, scientists have found and named only about $1\frac{1}{2}$ million. "Species," says Dr. Lovejoy, "are disappearing before we have a chance to learn how they might benefit the rest of the planet."

5   Thousands of kinds of tropical plants could help feed a growing world population. About four out of every ten prescription medicines come from ingredients found in plants. Some animals also provide medicines.

6   "It's natural for species to become extinct over millions of years," says Dr. Lovejoy. "What's *un*natural is that humans are speeding up the process many times over."

7   People are doing this in four main ways: destroying wildlife habitats, overhunting, introducing new species that endanger native wildlife, and polluting the environment. These activities affect all species in one way or another. "All life is interconnected," cautions Dr. Lovejoy.

8   Is there time to prevent disaster? Just barely, say scientists. Worldwide action will be difficult and costly. But scientists agree that action must be taken—quickly. The clock is ticking. . . .

Four Threats to Wildlife

POLLUTION

1   Wind and rain spread poisons across the land and through the oceans. Some poisons take years to do their damage. The peregrine falcon almost disappeared because of DDT, a pest-killing chemical sprayed from airplanes. Once in the environment, DDT remains a very long time. It enters the food chain and becomes more and more concentrated as larger animals eat smaller ones. It causes birds of prey to lay thin-shelled eggs that break when the parents sit on them. After the United States banned DDT in 1972, more peregrine chicks began hatching. Now, slowly, the birds are making a comeback.

HABITAT LOSS

2   Most people have never heard of the Texas poppy mallow. This plant grows only in a few places in Texas, and only where there is a deep layer of sand. Now the mallow is in danger of disappearing. Construction companies that use sand for building have destroyed much of its habitat. The plant faces an additional threat from ranchers who plow it under to plant grass for cattle. When a plant disappears, animals that depend on it directly for food or shelter also suffer. In turn, species that depend on such animals are affected. All life, scientists say, is interrelated.

OVERHUNTING

3   Many people in Asia believe powdered rhino horn is powerful medicine. In parts of the Middle East, a dagger with a rhino-horn handle symbolizes power. Such traditions result in tremendous pressure to harvest more and more rhino horns. A single rhino horn brings a poacher as much as $1,125. In some of the African countries where black rhinos live, that's what an average worker earns in two years. The profits are so high that black rhino hunting continues in spite of laws against it. The species is now endangered. Other animals endangered through overhunting include the blue whale, the cheetah, the grizzly bear, and the mountain gorilla.

INTRODUCTION OF NEW SPECIES

4   When Europeans first saw the animals of Australia, they were astounded. The animals didn't look like those at home. Many were marsupials—pouched mammals—like the rabbit-eared bandicoot. Australian animals soon got some surprises—unpleasant ones—of their own. The settlers brought in new species that competed for food and living space. Continents away from any natural enemies, the newcomers quickly multiplied, upsetting the balance among native species. Foxes hunted and killed bandicoots for food. Rabbits took over bandicoot burrows. Now, in its native land, the bandicoot struggles to survive.

A CLOUDED FUTURE

Clearing of Asian land for farms has destroyed much of the forest where clouded leopards once lived. Poaching—illegal hunting—adds to the cats' problems. Some leopards still survive in remote hideaways, but for how long?

A SYMBOL NEARLY LOST

In 1782, when the eagle became the symbol of the United States, many thousands nested in all parts of North America. Some 200 years later, only 1,500 pairs remained outside Alaska. The main reason: poisoning by DDT. With DDT banned in the U.S., the eagles, like the peregrine falcons, are slowly increasing in number.

THE TOLL ON TORTOISES

In the 1800s sailors stopped at Ecuador's Galápagos Islands to stock up on food—giant tortoises. While the ships lay at anchor, cats and rats came ashore. They did more harm than the sailors. By eating eggs and hatchlings, the introduced animals gradually reduced the tortoise population from 250,000 to 15,000.

INNOCENT VICTIM

Hunting almost wiped out the black-footed ferret. Yet the ferret was not the hunted animal; the prairie dog was. For centuries the two animals lived in the same burrow systems on the North American prairie. Prairie dogs ate grass, and ferrets ate prairie dogs. Then ranchers who needed the grass for cattle waged war on prairie dogs. The result: fewer prairie dogs and near extinction for the ferrets.

IDENTIFYING MAIN IDEAS

Summarize the main idea of each paragraph (from the article on pages 106–107) in one sentence. Then in small groups, compare your answers.

Paragraph 1: _____

Paragraph 2: _____

Paragraph 3: _____

Paragraph 4: _____

Paragraph 5: _____

Paragraph 6: _____

Paragraph 7: _____

Paragraph 8: _____

FINDING SUPPORT FOR MAIN IDEAS

The following statements contain quotes from the article. In your own words explain what the author means, and answer the questions.

1. "It's the tiny species that really run the planet," says Dr. Thomas Lovejoy. What four examples does the author give to support his point?

   a. _____

   b. _____

   c. _____

   d. _____

2. "All life, scientists say, is interrelated." Find an example in the article that proves this point.

   _____

   _____

3. "It's natural for species to become extinct over millions of years. What's *un*natural is that humans are speeding up the process many times over." In what four ways are humans speeding up the process?

   a. _____   c. _____

   b. _____   d. _____

**EXAMINING
EFFECTS**

1. Many of our actions have had a negative effect on the environment. Describe what happened in each of the following situations and identify the effect it had on other species.

a. Sailors stopped at the Galápagos Islands to stock up on food.

_____

_____

b. Farmers started using DDT.

_____

_____

c. Ranchers planted grass for their cattle.

_____

_____

d. Asian land was cleared for farms.

_____

_____

e. Construction companies in Texas used sand for building.

_____

_____

f. European settlers brought in new species of animals to Australia.

_____

_____

(continued on the next page)

2. How can old traditions result in overhunting? Give two specific examples from the article.

a. _____

_____

b. _____

_____

3. The author mentions four ways that humans are speeding up the process of extinction. Which of the four ways is responsible for the death of each of the following kinds of animals?

a. leopards: _____

b. eagles: _____

c. tortoises: _____

d. black-footed ferrets: _____

EXAMINING SOLUTIONS

The author mentions three ways that we can prevent pollution of the environment and endangerment of wildlife. Identify the three ways, and discuss the effectiveness of each one. Can you think of any others?

a. _____

b. _____

c. _____

WORD FORMS

Complete the sentences with the correct word. Change the given words to their plural form where necessary.

1. **solvable, solution, solve**

a. One way to _____ the problem of air pollution is to produce cans that pollute less.

b. Are the world's environmental problems _____?

c. Some people think that solar cars are the perfect _____ to the problems of air pollution.

2. **experiment, experimenting, experimentally, experimental**

   a. Several new methods of increasing the food supply are still in _____ stages.

   b. Some people don't believe in _____ on animals.

   c. Automakers are continuing to _____ with ways to burn cleaner fuels.

   d. New kinds of crops are being grown _____.

3. **science, scientific, scientist, scientifically**

   a. _____ are investigating ways to improve methods of food production.

   b. This report is not _____; it is based on one person's theory.

   c. Ever since he was a child, he has been interested in _____.

   d. The information we have is _____ correct.

4. **conserve, conservation, conservationist**

   a. Everyone should try to _____ our natural resources.

   b. The _____ of our rain forests is very important.

   c. Dr. Thomas Lovejoy is a _____ with the Smithsonian Institute.

5. **destroy, destruction, destructive, indestructible**

   a. The _____ of trees can cause erosion.

   b. We should try to protect, not _____, our wildlife.

   c. It is a mistake to think our earth is _____.

   d. Acid rain and pollution are _____ forces that hurt the environment.

The birds of the world are disappearing. Two-thirds of all species of birds are on the decline, and 1,000 species are threatened with extinction.

6. **produce, production, product, productive, productivity**

   a. The _____ of meat is not an efficient use of grains.

   b. We need to _____ more food in order to feed our increasing population.

   c. The meeting was very _____; we came up with a lot of good ideas.

   d. Scientists are trying to increase the _____ of our farmland.

   e. Some companies are now making _____ that use recycled paper.

7. **globe, global, globally**

   a. We have to begin thinking _____ about environmental problems.

   b. Hunger and overpopulation are _____ problems.

   c. Nations around the _____ are concerned with the state of our environment.

8. **develop, developing, developed, development**

   a. Hunger is a more severe problem in _____ countries.

   b. We need to _____ disease-resistant crops.

   c. The _____ of better farming techniques is a step in the right direction.

   d. People living in _____ countries tend to eat more meat.

9. **pollute, pollutant, pollution**

   a. There will soon be more cars that make little or no _____.

   b. Zero-emission vehicles do not _____ the air at all.

   c. Vehicles cause 56 percent of cancer-causing air _____.

JUST FOR FUN

Look at the word *environmental*. **It contains thirteen letters. Using only these thirteen letters, try to make as many other words as you can. You may not use the same letter twice unless it appears twice in the word. Also, you cannot use proper names or foreign words. Write the words here as you think of them.**

_____   _____

_____   _____

_____   _____

_____   _____

_____

POSTREADING DISCUSSION QUESTIONS

1. What do you think is the biggest environmental problem that your country faces? What, if anything, is being done to solve it?

2. In what ways can each of us be friendlier to our environment? Make a list and share it with your classmates.

3. Read and discuss the following quote. Do you agree or disagree with it?

> The emergence of intelligence, I am convinced, tends to unbalance the ecology. In other words, intelligence is the great polluter. It is not until a creature begins to manage its environment that nature is thrown into disorder.[1]

4. When a Russian cosmonaut viewed the Earth from space, he wrote, "It does not matter what country you look at. We are all Earth's children and we should treat her as our mother." How are his ideas similar to those of the Native Americans?

READER'S JOURNAL

Write for ten to twenty minutes in your Reader's Journal about an environmental issue that interests you.

[1] Clifford D. Simak, *Macmillan Dictionary of Quotations* (New York: Macmillan, 1987), 189.

READER'S JOURNAL

Date: _____

GETTING DOWN TO BUSINESS

Selections

In this unit, you will read about several aspects of business. Before you read the articles, use the following questions to get yourself thinking about the business of business.

Think about and then discuss the following questions.

1. Where do you think the scene in the cartoon below is taking place? What clues made you realize where the people are? What is the woman trying to sell? Did the cartoon make you laugh? If so, what do you think is funny about it?

2. Think about the last time you went shopping. Did you buy only things that you needed, or did you also buy things that caught your attention and you decided you wanted? Did you buy anything on impulse at the last minute? What is your usual buying pattern?

3. How are you influenced by advertising? Do you take advantage of sales, special offers, and coupons? Are you loyal to certain brands? If so, which ones?

4. Do you have business experience that lets you think about these and other questions from a businessperson's point of view as well as a consumer's point of view? If so, what kind of business experience do you have?

DICK WRIGHT reprinted by permission of UFS, Inc.

Blue jeans are very popular with people of all ages and nationalities. Look around your classroom. How many people are wearing jeans? In **Levi's Gold** you will read about Levi Strauss, the man who first introduced jeans.

BEFORE YOU READ

PREREADING ACTIVITY

1. What are some of the most popular brands of blue jeans in your country? Is Levi's a popular brand in your country?

2. What are some places where it is appropriate to wear jeans in your country? Are there some places where you wouldn't wear jeans? For example, would you wear jeans to work, school, a nice restaurant, church?

3. Before you read the article, discuss the meaning of the following words and phrases with your classmates:

   gold rush   patent   canvas
   prospector   peddle   entrepreneur

FIRST READING

SKIMMING

Read the article one time quickly, and look for the main idea. That is, skim the article.

● ●

Levi's Gold

D O R O T H Y   S L A T E

1   When the clipper ship sailed through California's Golden Gate[1] that March day in 1853, twenty-four-year-old Levi Strauss rushed to the deck, eager to see San Francisco. The Gold Rush[2], started in 1848, still drew men by the thousands to seek their fortunes. Strauss was one of them.

2   Six years earlier, he had left Bavaria in Germany to escape unfair laws against Jews and to join his older brothers Jonas and Louis in New York. They taught him English and told him peddling was an

---

[1]Golden Gate The entrance to San Francisco Bay in northern California from the Pacific Ocean.
[2]Gold Rush Gold was discovered in California in the late 1840s. As a result, many people rushed to California, hoping to find gold and become rich.

honorable occupation in the United States. Now he faced a new challenge. In his baggage were goods to sell. His brothers had helped select them in New York before he left on his long voyage around Cape Horn to California. Gold miners were sure to need thread, needles, scissors, thimbles, and rolls of canvas cloth for tents and wagon covers.

3 As Strauss looked toward the city, he saw several small boats approaching the ship. When they came close, some of their passengers clamored for news from the East. Others climbed aboard to see what merchandise the ship had brought. In a short while, Strauss had sold almost everything he had brought with him. Only the rolls of canvas remained.

4 Stepping ashore, he saw a bustling city with many "stores" that were merely tents or shanties. Among the ironworks, billiard-table manufacturers, dry-goods stores, breweries, and hundreds of saloons stood some stranded ships serving as hotels.

5 With gold dust from his sales aboard ship, Strauss bought a cart. He loaded his rolls of canvas and pushed the cart along wood-planked sidewalks. He parked on Montgomery Street, waiting for miners to pass by.

6 A prospector stopped to look at his canvas.

7 "It's for tenting," Strauss explained.

8 "Shoulda brought pants," the prospector told him. "Pants don't wear worth a hoot in the diggin's. Can't get a pair strong enough to last."

9 Instantly, the young entrepreneur sought out a tailor and created the first pair of jeans. Pleased with them, his customer later strutted around San Francisco. "Doggone, if a man ever had a pair of pants strong as Levi's before," he said.

10 The demand for "Levi's" grew so fast that Strauss could hardly

keep up with it. When the brown canvas was gone, he switched to a sturdy fabric, *serge de Nîmes,* from Nîmes, France. The name was quickly shortened to "denim," and Strauss adopted the indigo blue familiar today.

11 Levi's brothers Jonas and Louis were his partners, as was David Stern, who had married Levi's sister Fanny. They decided to call their firm Levi Strauss & Company, agreeing that Levi was the "business head" in the family. Years went by, and the business grew.

12 Then, in July 1872, a letter arrived from Jacob W. Davis, a tailor in Reno. The letter explained that he was now reinforcing pants pocket corners with copper rivets. Rivets strengthened the seams, which tore out when miners and other workers stuffed their pockets with gold nuggets and tools.

13 Davis was flooded with orders but worried that someone would steal his idea. If Levi Strauss & Company would take out a patent in his name, Davis would give them half the right to sell the riveted clothing.

14 Strauss immediately saw the profit potential. Instead of nine or ten dollars a dozen, the riveted pants could bring thirty-six dollars—just for adding a penny's worth of metal. It was a good risk.

15 The U.S. Patent Office took its time in granting Strauss a patent. It took ten months and many revisions and amendments before the Patent Office agreed that the idea of riveted pockets was unusual enough to be patented.

16 When Davis moved his family to San Francisco, Strauss put him in charge of production. Soon a force of sixty women stitched Levi's on a piecework basis. The orange thread still used today was an attempt to match the copper rivets. Another still-used trademark is the leather label featuring two teamsters whipping a pair of horses trying to tear apart the riveted pants.

17 Successful in business, Levi Strauss still found time to participate in many civic organizations and was well liked in San Francisco's business community. He never married, saying, "I am a bachelor, and I fancy on that account I need to work more, for my entire life is my business."

18 Although he had no children of his own, Strauss established many scholarships at the University of California, and when he died in 1902, he left money to Protestant, Catholic, and Jewish orphanages. He left the business to his sister Fanny's children.

19 Levi Strauss found gold not in streams or mines, but in fulfilling an everyday need. Today presidents, movie stars, and millions of other people wear Levi's and other brands of jeans, clothing created by an entrepreneur who responded to the needs of the market.

IDENTIFYING THE MAIN IDEA

Circle the letter of the statement that best expresses the main idea of the passage.

a. Gold miners bought Levi's pants because they were strong and durable.

b. Levi Strauss was able to make his fortune in jeans by responding to the needs of the market.

c. Levi was the "business head" of the Strauss family.

d. Levi Strauss was successful in business, but he still found time to participate in civic organizations.

SECOND READING

Now reread "Levi's Gold" and do the exercises that follow.

HOW WELL DID YOU READ?

Read the following statements. If a statement is true, write *T* on the line. If it is false, write *F*.

_____ 1. Levi's pants became popular very quickly.

_____ 2. Levi brought canvas cloth to San Francisco to sell pants to the gold miners.

_____ 3. Levi Strauss & Co. was a family business.

_____ 4. The U.S. Patent Office quickly granted the patent for riveted pockets.

_____ 5. Levi thought of using copper rivets to reinforce pocket corners.

RECALLING INFORMATION

HOW MUCH CAN YOU REMEMBER?

Complete the paragraph with information from the article. See how much you can do without referring to the article. You do not have to use the exact words from the article as long as the idea is correct.

Levi Strauss went to _____ in 1853 in search of

_____, but ended up making his fortune in

_____. He realized that a good way to make money was to

make and sell _____ _____ that were suited

for a _____ lifestyle. His new business was very

_____, and soon many people were buying his

_____. In 1872, he made another good business decision;

he added _____ to his pant's pocket corners. This

increased his _____ even more. Today, jeans are as

_____ as ever. All types of people, including

_____, _____, and even

_____, can be seen wearing Levi jeans.

ORGANIZING INFORMATION

Here is a list of important events in Levi Strauss's life. Put them in correct time order by numbering them from 1 to 7.

_____ a. Levi sold his first pair of pants.

_____ b. Levi left Germany to join his brothers in New York.

_____ c. He got a patent for riveted pockets.

_____ d. He moved to San Francisco.

_____ e. He began using blue denim to make his pants.

_____ f. Levi Strauss & Company was established.

_____ g. He left his business to his sister's children.

FIGURE IT OUT

VOCABULARY IN CONTEXT

Without using your dictionary, write an approximate definition or a synonym for the highlighted words in the following sentences. Then compare your answers with those of your classmates.

1. _The Gold Rush, started in 1848, still **drew** men by the thousands to seek their fortunes._

_____

_____

2. _Pleased with [his pants], his customer later **strutted** around San Francisco._

_____

_____

(continued on the next page)

3. *The demand for "Levi's" grew so fast that Strauss could hardly **keep up** with it.*

_____

_____

4. *When the brown canvas was gone, he **switched** to a sturdy fabric, serge de Nîmes, from Nîmes, France.*

_____

_____

FYi

In 1982, AT&T made $7.6 billion in profit. This was the greatest net profit ever made by a corporation in a twelve-month period.

5. *Rivets strengthened the seams, which tore out when miners and other workers **stuffed** their pockets with gold nuggets and tools.*

_____

_____

6. *Davis was **flooded** with orders but worried that someone would steal his idea.*

_____

_____

7. *Today presidents, movie stars, and millions of other people wear Levi's and other **brands** of jeans.*

_____

_____

TALK IT OVER

DISCUSSION QUESTIONS

1. Levi Strauss sold his first pair of pants in 1853. Today his idea for practical pants is still influencing the fashion world. Why do you think jeans are still so popular?

2. In the last paragraph the author states, "Levi Strauss found gold not in streams or mines, but in fulfilling an everyday need." What was the need that he fulfilled? What do you think made him such a successful entrepreneur? What are the qualities that make someone successful in business?

Our sense of smell can influence our behavior in many ways. Decisions about what we eat, what we wear, who we are attracted to, and even what we buy can be influenced by smell. In **Smells Sell!,** you will read about how advertisers use the sense of smell to increase sales.

BEFORE YOU READ

MAKING PREDICTIONS

1. Read the title, subtitle, and headings of this article. Also, look at the picture. What do you think the article will be about? Write your prediction on the lines provided.

_____

_____

_____

2. Now read the first and last two paragraphs of the article. Can you make your prediction more specific?

_____

_____

_____

3. Finally, read the first sentence of each paragraph. Do you want to change your prediction at all? If so, write your new prediction below.

_____

_____

_____

READING THE ARTICLE

Now read the whole article, and do the exercises that follow.

Smells Sell!

Melinda Crow

Scent Experts Lead You by the Nose

1   You're standing in the cereal aisle at the grocery store, searching for your favorite brand. Suddenly, you catch a whiff of chocolate-chip cookies. Your mouth begins to water. You forget about cereal and head for the bakery section.

2   Guess what? You just walked into a trap—an odor trap! The yummy smell was fake. The odor was cooked up by scientists in a lab, then spread by the store's owners to lure you to the bakery section.

DOLLARS AND SCENTS

3   For years, scientists have been studying the special powers of smells. It seems that our noses and our brains are very closely connected. When you smell something, the odor goes up your nose to smelling zones. From here, sense cells send nerve messages to your brain telling it what you smelled.

4   More than our other four senses, our sense of smell changes our mood and helps us remember things. If you were told to think about popcorn, you'd probably recall its smell. And then you might remember the movie you saw while eating it. Our sense of smell also helps us sniff out danger—like the smell of smoke. And it can make your mouth water from just one whiff of food.

5   If smell is so powerful, say store owners, then maybe it can also sell products. So businesses have begun spending thousands of dollars to scent entire stores. Fake scents are being used to lead customers by the nose. These bogus odors help to get people inside and put them in the mood to buy. They even make customers remember the store later, so they'll come back for more.

6   Some business people predict that in 10 years, store smells will be as common as the soft music stores often play to put shoppers in a good mood.

HIDDEN PELLETS AND GOO

7   J'Amy Owens designs stores for a living. To keep up with the new trend in store odors, she recently began including "fragrance planning" as part of her store design. She believes each store should have its own special smell.

8   For a kids' clothing store in San Francisco, CA, for example, she's using the smell of cinnamon and hot apple spice. She hopes shoppers will end up thinking these kids' clothes are as American as apple pie!

9 Sometimes Owens gets strange requests. "The owner of a fast-food restaurant wanted to know if I could scent the speaker at the drive-up window," she says.

10 Owens spreads the store scents secretly, using little balls soaked in fragrance. She hides them in light fixtures and heating pipes. If that doesn't give off enough odor, she puts in a small heater. This warms up the fragrance. A fan then spreads this smell throughout the store.

11 Other stores use computer-controlled machines to carry the smell out through the store's air vents. Getting the right amount of odor in the air can be tricky. When Steven Schultz first started using peach fragrance in his discount store in Louisville, KY, the whole place ended up smelling like a peach warehouse.

SOMETHING SMELLS FISHY

12 Dr. Alan Hirsch designs smells for businesses. He says that it doesn't take a whole lot of smell to affect you. Store owners can lure you to the candy aisle—even if you don't realize you're smelling candy. This idea scares a lot of people. Groups that protect the rights of shoppers are upset. They say the stores are using a kind of brainwashing, which they call "smell-washing."

13 "It's pretty sleazy," says Mark Silbergeld. He runs an organization that checks out products for consumers.

14 The scientists hired to design the scents disagree. "There's mellow background music, there's neon lighting, there are all sorts of bells and jingles being used," says Dr. Hirsch. "Why not smells?"

15 One reason why not, says Silbergeld, is that some people are allergic to certain scents pumped into products or stores.

16 But there's a whole other side to this debate. Do the smells really work? So far there is little proof one way or the other. But Dr. Hirsch has run some interesting experiments.

17 In one of Hirsch's experiments, 31 volunteers were led into a sneaker store that smelled slightly like flowers. Later, another group shopped in the same store, but with no flower odor.

18 Dr. Hirsch found that 84 percent of the shoppers were more likely to buy the sneakers in the flower-scented room. But Hirsch found out something even stranger.

19 "Whether the volunteers liked the flower scent or not didn't matter," Hirsch says. "Some reported that they hated the smell. But they still were more likely to buy the shoes in the scented room."

WHO KNOWS THE FUTURE?

20 Using smells to sell products isn't new. In 1966, a company added lemon fragrance to its dish detergent. They wanted people to think the soap contained "natural" cleaners. It worked! Today, businesses spend over a billion dollars a year just on product odor.

21 Some companies have already discovered ways to make microwaveable foods smell good before they're cooked. They scent the packages. Smell for yourself. Next time you pop a bag of microwave popcorn, smell the bag

before you put it in the microwave. Chances are, it already smells like popped corn.

22   New uses for smells are being created every day. One bank, for example, gives customers coupons advertising car loans. To get people to take out a loan, bank officials hope to coat these coupons with the fresh leather smell of a new car.

23   In Australia, companies are putting sweat odor on unpaid bills. Since some people sweat when they're scared, this smell might remind them of when they are frightened. And they'll pay the bills right away.

24   What lies ahead for our noses? Smell scientists are working on some outrageous ideas. Would you believe TV sets that produce smells? Or how about odor diets? Certain food smells will fool your stomach into thinking it's full.

25   Alarm clocks will scent your bedroom with an aroma designed to wake you up. Scientists are even working on ways to keep garbage from stinking. And researchers expect scents to one day help students make more sense of what they're learning.

HOW WELL DID YOU READ?

TRUE /FALSE

Read the statements that follow. If a statement is true, write _T_ on the line. If it is false, write _F_.

_____ 1. The sense of smell can change your mood and help you remember things.

_____ 2. Because the sense of smell is so powerful, some businesses have begun using it to sell products.

_____ 3. In the future, store smells might be as common as soft music.

_____ 4. It takes a large amount of a certain smell to affect a customer.

_____ 5. It is always easy to get the right amount of odor in the air.

_____ 6. Some groups and organizations oppose the idea of using smells to attract and influence customers.

_____ 7. There is a lot of evidence supporting the idea that smells influence customer behavior.

_____ 8. Using smells to sell products is a new development in marketing.

_____ 9. New uses for smells are being developed all the time.

SUPPORTING MAIN IDEAS

USING EXAMPLES

Find examples in the article to support each of the following ideas.

1. *More than our other four senses, our sense of smell changes our mood and helps us remember things.*

_____

_____

2. *. . . . each store should have its own special smell.*

_____

_____

3. *Getting the right amount of odor in the air can be tricky.*

_____

_____

4. *Using smells to sell products isn't new.*

_____

_____

5. *Some companies have already discovered ways to make microwaveable foods smell good before they're cooked.*

_____

_____

6. *New uses for smells are being created every day.*

_____

_____

BUILDING VOCABULARY SKILLS

List all the words or phrases from the article that have to do with smell. Try to find as many as you can.

_____

_____

_____

_____

_____

_____

_____

_____

FIGURE IT OUT

IDIOMS AND EXPRESSIONS

An **idiom** is a phrase that has a special meaning. The meaning of the phrase as a whole is different from the meanings of the individual words in the phrase. For example, in the sentence, "I'm sure David was pulling my leg when he told me he had won the lottery," the idiom *pulling my leg* means teasing me.

An **expression** is also a group of words with a special meaning. For example, in the sentence, "She hopes shoppers will end up thinking these kids' clothes are as American as apple pie," the expression *as American as apple pie* means that something is very American.

"Smells Sell!" is filled with idioms and expressions. Circle the letter of the word or phrase that best describes the idiom.

1. *You forget about cereal and **head for** the bakery section.*

   a. walk toward
   b. point your head at
   c. remember

2. *You just **walked into a trap**—an odor trap!*

   a. avoided
   b. got tricked
   c. smelled

3. *The odor was **cooked up** by scientists in a lab. . . .*

   a. sold
   b. invented
   c. discussed

4. *Fake scents are being used **to lead customers by the nose**.*

   a. direct customers
   b. get rid of customers
   c. discourage customers

5. *He runs an organization that **checks out** products for customers.*

   a. removes
   b. leaves
   c. investigates

6. But Hirsch ***found out*** something even stranger.

   a. wrote about
   b. discovered
   c. examined

TALK IT OVER

DISCUSSION
QUESTIONS

1. Consider again how sensitive you are to smells. Do you think it's realistic to think that artificial smells can influence your buying behavior?

2. "Synthetic fragrances just add more chemicals to the chemical soup. It's an outrage." (Dr. Albert Robbins, environmental medicine specialist[1]) What do you think Dr. Robbins means? Do you think indoor air pollution is a major health risk?

3. Do you use incense, cologne, aftershave lotion, perfume, or pot pourri? Which ones? Do you use them often?

[1]*The Environmental Magazine* (July/August 1993), 10.

The next reading is a book review called **The Gender-Spender Gap**. The book reviewed is *Why Women Pay More*. The purpose of a book review is to give a critical analysis and summary of the book. If the review is positive, it may make people want to buy the book.

1. Before you read the book review, discuss these words and expressions with your teacher and classmates.

bargain, bargaining	surcharge
discrepancy	sticker price
negotiate	trends
savvy	perils
abuses	scams
fraud	outrages

2. Look at the cover of *Why Women Pay More*. What technique does the author use to get you interested in reading the book?

_____

_____

_____

_____

Read the book review one time quickly and identify the statement that best expresses the main idea of *Why Women Pay More*.

1. *Why Women Pay More* compares the salaries of men and women and provides research showing that women usually make less money.

2. *Why Women Pay More* examines the process of buying a new car and offers some ways to make it easier.

3. *Why Women Pay More* discusses situations where women pay more than men for the same things and suggests ways women can get more for their money.

The Gender-Spender Gap

PETER NYE

WHY WOMEN PAY MORE

HOW TO AVOID
MARKETPLACE PERILS

Health Abuses
Financial Scams
Consumer Fraud
And other outrages...

Frances Cerra Whittelsey
Introduction by Ralph Nader

1 Women pay more—and get less—than men for car insurance, haircuts, dry cleaning, and surgical operations. In *Why Women Pay More*, Frances Cerra Whittelsey, a veteran consumer affairs reporter who spent 15 years with *The New York Times* and *Newsday*, surveys a number of important consumer areas and suggests how women can get more for their money.

2 She points out that women buy about half the cars sold each year, yet pay more than men. White women pay $150 more for the identical car than a white man after they both went through a rehearsed process of bargaining. African-American men paid $400 more, and African-American women suffered the most—they were offered a price averaging $800 higher than white men.

3 "Furthermore, certain industries have simply charged us more for items and services identical to those provided to men," Whittelsey says. For example, women pay a surcharge for clothes alterations, which typically are included when men buy suits. "These 'traditional' pricing practices have been going on for so long, in fact, that most women have never even noticed the discrepancy."

4 As if these problems aren't enough, women often are paid 60 to 75 percent of what men earn for the same job. Whittelsey cites a study that shows women earn an average of 74 cents for every dollar that men are paid.

5 Women are also less likely than men to realize that a car sticker price is negotiable, she suggests. "The same may be true for other items like computers, telephone systems, appliances, home improvements, TVs and stereos—the list goes on and on," she writes. To avoid marketplace perils, she encourages women to negotiate for products and services.

Read the review of *Why Women Pay More* again more carefully. Try not to use your dictionary, and don't worry if you can't understand every word.

Answer the following questions.

1. What example does the author give to show that some industries charge women more than men for services?

_____

_____

_____

2. How does the author of the book support her claim that women are often paid less than men for the same job?

_____

_____

_____

_____

3. In addition to cars, what other products may have prices that can be negotiated? Find several examples from the review.

_____

_____

_____

_____

4. Do you think this is a positive or negative review of the book? Why? Give specific examples from the review to support your answer.

_____

_____

_____

_____

Nothing but the Truth discusses one of the latest trends in advertising: the marketing of products that are good for you and safe for the environment.

BEFORE YOU
READ

PREREADING
QUESTIONS

1. Would you be more likely to buy something that you think is safer for the environment? Why or why not? What about products that are supposed to be healthier? Does this claim have an effect on what you buy?

2. Do you read the labels on products? Do they influence your purchasing decisions? If so, how do they affect your decisions? If not, why don't they affect them?

3. The first sentence of this article says, "For manufacturers and advertisers, the marketing of 'ecofriendly' and 'healthy, all-natural' products can mean big profits." Why do you think manufacturers and advertisers want to market their products as ecologically friendly and healthy? Can you guess why these kinds of products mean big profits?

FIRST READING   **Read the article one time quickly, and do the exercise that follows.**

● ●

Nothing but the Truth

S E A N   M C C O L L U M

For manufacturers and advertisers, the marketing of "ecofriendly" and "healthy, all-natural" products can mean big profits. But how can the consumer tell fact from fancy?

1   Pick an aisle, any aisle, and roll your shopping cart along the supermarket shelves. What words do you see? "Fat free!" "Ozone safe!" "Lite!" "100% Recycled!" "High-Fiber!" "Earth-friendly!" Welcome to the wonderful world of green and health-conscious marketing, the very latest in consumer advertising.

2   Americans have always expressed their passions and concerns through the products they buy. "I Shop, Therefore I Am," as the bumpersticker says. And for the last five years or so, no two issues have been of more concern to the American consumer than the environment and health. Bombarded with endless reports about the threat of global warming, the destruction of the

ozone layer, how fatty foods damage the heart, and why sugar isn't good for you, shoppers have begun paying closer attention to the products they buy. Poll after opinion poll shows that Americans are eager to buy healthier and environmentally safer products—and pay more for them, if necessary.

3 Manufacturers got the message loud and clear. Never slow to spot and capitalize on trends, America's biggest advertisers jumped on the eco-health bandwagon. But while some companies made genuine improvements in their products to attract the green consumer, others just added a few catchy words to their packages.

4 Tom's of Maine is one company that's done well with genuinely environmentally sensitive products. Tom's toothpaste boxes, and boxes for other items, are all made with 100 percent recycled paper. Plastic bottles are all made with polyethylene—an easily recyclable plastic. The company also sells refills of its deodorants so customers can reuse the plastic bottles.

5 Most manufacturers don't go to these lengths, though that doesn't stop them from making exaggerated claims about the environmental benefits of their wares. Although a writing tablet or a roll of computer paper may say it's "recycled," it may contain as little as 50 percent wastepaper. A hairspray that boasts it contains "No CFCs"—which destroy the earth's ozone layer—may use another ozone-eater, trichloroethane, instead. A shampoo manufacturer may claim its plastic bottle is recyclable, but if it's made of polyvinyl chloride it's not. Apparently, the attitude of some manufacturers is: What you don't know won't hurt you.

Fast and Loose

6   Now, the federal government has started taking a close look at companies playing fast and loose with environmental claims. Last summer the Federal Trade Commission (FTC), the agency charged with protecting consumers from misleading advertising, issued guidelines on what environmental claims can and can't be made.

7   A recent case involved Mr. Coffee, the coffee-maker manufacturer. Mr. Coffee had put the following on its packages of coffee filters: "Here's Why Mr. Coffee Filters Are Better For Coffee Lovers and Nature Lovers—No Chlorine: Our exclusive paper is cleaned and whitened without using chlorine bleach, which has been found to create undesirable byproducts." The packaging also implied that the filters were made of recycled paper.

8   But according to Mary Engle, a staff attorney with the FTC, that's only part of the story. "In fact, the filters were bleached with chlorine dioxide, which is not the same as chlorine, but chlorine was still involved in the process," she says. "Undesirable byproducts were still being released into the environment. And the paper wasn't recycled."

9   In March, Mr. Coffee signed a settlement with the FTC, withdrawing the "chlorine-free" and "recycled paper" claims.

10   Until the FTC smokes out all the offenders, how are consumers to know if a manufacturer is stretching the truth? A new Washington, D.C.-based group called Green Seal may help. Green Seal has set itself up as an independent tester of "green" products. It's asking companies to voluntarily submit their goods to Green Seal for testing. If they meet the group's standards, then the companies will be allowed to place the Green Seal logo—a blue globe with a green checkmark—on their packaging.

Fanciful Claims

11   Although "green seals" may soon show up on shampoo bottles, there won't be a "health seal" arriving anytime soon to help clear up the confusion about which foods are good for you. With more and more Americans concerned with eating healthy, more and more food manufacturers are making fanciful claims about the nutritional value of their products. Usually such claims try to make a connection between the presence of a nutrient, like oat bran, or the absence of a substance, like fat, with a health benefit. Thus the familiar claim that "low-fat" foods are better for the heart.

12 But starting this month, manufacturers who claim their edibles will make you healthier, or use terms such as "lite," "low-fat," and "high in dietary fiber," had better know exactly what they're talking about. That's when strict new guidelines issued by the Food and Drug Administration (FDA)—the watchdog of the food industry—go into effect.

13 Until now, there's been little control over what food producers could put on product labels or into advertisements. That led to a "free-for-all" of health claims, as one analyst put it. The great oat-bran hype is a good example. A few years ago, oat bran became the rage among many consumers because of its high fiber content. Some studies indicated a connection between high-fiber diets and a reduced risk of cancer. But many cereal makers sprinkled a minuscule amount of oat bran into their cereal, truthfully put "Contains Oat Bran!" on the box, and snickered all the way to the bank.

14 Under the new FDA guidelines, that kind of labeling is forbidden. Only health claims supported by strong scientific evidence will be permitted. And only products with "significant amounts" will be allowed to boast of it on the box.

15 The FDA is also cracking down on other common marketing catchwords, like "low sodium" and "low calorie." Under the new guidelines, foods must have less than 140 milligrams of sodium or less than 40 calories per serving to make these claims. A "lite" beer had better contain one-third fewer calories than its "non-lite" version, or it's lights out for that particular type of advertising.

16 The FTC and FDA guidelines should help restore some consumer confidence about trusting labels and ads. But, of course, if there's an angle or a loophole, some advertiser will find it. For the smart shopper, the old adage still holds true: *Caveat emptor*—Let the buyer beware.

● ●

HOW WELL DID YOU READ?

Read the following statements. If a statement is true, write _T_ on the line provided. If it is false, write _F_. Then locate and identify the paragraph in the article that contains the information that helped you make your decision.

_____ 1. The products Americans buy are an expression of their feelings and concerns. (¶ _____)

_____ 2. Some manufacturers believe that what consumers don't know won't hurt them. (¶ _____)

_____ 3. In the past, there was a lot of control over what information could be put on labels and into advertisements. (¶ _____)

_____ 4. Products that have a Green Seal logo on them are environmentally sensitive. (¶ _____)

_____ 5. American consumers are very concerned about buying healthier and environmentally safer products. (¶ _____)

_____ 6. The FTC has issued stricter guidelines on environmental claims made by manufacturers. (¶ _____)

_____ 7. Health seals will soon be placed on foods that are good for you. (¶ _____)

_____ 8. The FDA plans to issue strict new guidelines governing what food producers can put on their labels. (¶ _____)

_____ 9. All companies have made real improvements in their products. (¶ _____)

_____ 10. In the future, health claims used in advertising will have to be supported by strong scientific evidence. (¶ _____)

SECOND READING

Now read the article again more carefully.

CHALLENGE ACTIVITY

UNDERSTANDING IDIOMS

These sentences from the article contain idiomatic expressions (highlighted in bold). Carefully read these original sentences and the sentences *a* and *b* that follow each one. Circle the letter of the sentence that is closest in meaning to the original one.

1. *Never slow to spot and capitalize on trends, America's biggest advertisers* **jumped on the eco-health bandwagon.**

   a. When advertisers saw that Americans were concerned about environment and health issues, they started showing an interest in them, too.
   b. The big advertisers were the first group to become concerned about ecological and health issues.

(continued on the next page)

2. *Most manufacturers **don't go to these lengths,** though that doesn't stop them from making exaggerated claims about the environmental benefits of their wares.*

   a. Most manufacturers aren't concerned with making products that appeal to environmentally conscious consumers.

   b. Most manufacturers don't go to extremes in making their products environmentally sensitive, but they still make exaggerated claims about them.

3. *Until the FTC **smokes out** all the offenders, how are consumers to know if a manufacturer is **stretching the truth**?*

   a. The FTC needs to hide the offenders to keep consumers from knowing which ones are telling the truth.

   b. Until the FTC identifies the offenders, consumers won't know which manufacturers are exaggerating their claims.

4. *But many cereal makers sprinkled a minuscule amount of oat bran into their cereal, truthfully put "Contains Oat Bran!" on the box, and **snickered all the way to the bank**.*

   a. By exaggerating the claim about containing oat bran, many cereal makers were able to make a lot of money.

   b. Many cereal makers tried to fool the public with their claims about oat bran but were not able to make much money.

5. *The FDA is also **cracking down** on other common marketing catchwords, like "low sodium" and "low calorie."*

   a. The FDA is becoming stricter about what kinds of words advertisers use.

   b. The FDA is trying to get rid of words such as "low sodium" and "low calorie."

ANALYZING THE PASSAGE

WRITING COMPREHENSION QUESTIONS

By this time, you have had a lot of experience answering questions about the readings in this book. Now it's your turn to write the questions. In this activity, you will have an opportunity to write questions for your classmates to answer. The procedure is as follows:

1. In small groups, discuss the article and decide which parts you want to ask questions about.

2. Write a rough draft of your questions. Try to include at least five multiple-choice questions, five discussion questions, and five vocabulary items. Try to think of other types of questions, such as matching and fill in the blank. Be creative!

3. Check your questions for proper sentence structure, grammar, spelling, and punctuation. After you revise and proofread your questions, write or type a final draft neatly on a clean sheet of paper. Be sure to write clear instructions and leave plenty of space on the paper for your classmates to write their answers.

4. Exchange papers with another group. Discuss and answer the questions, writing your final answers on the spaces provided.

5. Return the papers to the group that wrote the questions for their assessment of your answers.

APPLICATION OF INFORMATION

1. Look through several magazines and cut out ads that appeal to environmentally conscious consumers. Make a list of the words, expressions, and slogans the advertisers used to convince the public that their product is environmentally safe.

_____

_____

_____

_____

_____

2. Now cut out ads that target people who are concerned about their health. What catchwords and slogans do the advertisers use?

_____

_____

_____

_____

Coca-Cola products are sold in 197 countries around the world. 705 million servings of Coca-cola-owned soft drinks are sold per day worldwide. The country that serves the most eight-ounce servings of Coke per year per person is Mexico.

3. Bumper stickers, like advertising slogans, are a reflection of attitudes. The article mentions one bumper sticker that says, "I Shop, Therefore I Am." What do you think this message means?
What other bumper stickers have you seen? Are bumper stickers popular in your country?

141

JUST FOR FUN

CROSSWORD
PUZZLE

The words in the crossword puzzle are all from the exercises and activities you have worked through in this unit. Complete the puzzle using the clues provided. Then check your answers in the Answer Key on page 213.

ACROSS

1. another word for *buyer*
2. when we make more money than we spend, we make a _____
3. a trick that is played on someone in order to make money
4. opposite of a buyer
5. pressure that causes people to feel physically, mentally, or emotionally bad
6. something that causes extreme anger
7. denim pants
8. copper used to strengthen seams
9. to discuss the final price of an item
10. dishonest act or person
11. design or pattern used to identify a product
12. magazine used to sell and buy items
13. to have good practical understanding of a subject is to be _____ in that subject
14. the sense associated with using the nose
15. particular make or type of product
16. to have an excessive amount of something is to be _____ with something

DOWN

1. payment
2. average
3. to walk proudly
4. someone who spends is a _____
5. unpleasant smell
6. to be masculine or feminine is to be of one _____ or the other
7. technique or plan
8. government protection of an invention so it will not be copied
9. short, quick breaths through the nose in order to detect a smell
10. target market
11. to discuss in order to come to an agreement
12. difficult (in this article), but can also mean deceitful
13. catchy phrase used in advertising
14. to change
15. piece of paper or cloth that identifies a product
16. to attract (also means to pull)

**POSTREADING
DISCUSSION
QUESTIONS**

Below are several quotations about business. Read the quotes and discuss them, using information from the articles and your own experience.

1. "Don't forget until too late that the business of life is not business, but living." B. C. Forbes

   What do you think this quote means? Do you agree with Forbes's point of view? Do you know people who lead their lives as though they think work is all there is to life? What are some of the reasons people might do this? In English we call these people "workaholics." Are you one of these people?

2. The owner of a well-known department store is quoted as saying: "Half the money I spend on advertising is wasted, and the trouble is I don't know which half."

   Do you believe that one half of the money spent on advertising is wasted? Which half?

3. Business is concerned with persuading people to buy. As a result, a lot of money is spent on marketing, advertising, and promotion. A cosmetics tycoon is quoted as saying, "We don't sell lipstick, we buy customers."

   Do you think this is a negative view of human nature or a realistic one? Do you ever feel manipulated when you buy something? If so, when?

**READER'S
JOURNAL**

Write for ten to twenty minutes in your Reader's Journal on some aspect of business that interests you. Use as much information as you can from the readings to support your ideas.

READER'S JOURNAL

Date: _____

THE POWER OF MUSIC

Selections

In the past, you may have thought that the primary purpose of music was to entertain. As you read this unit, you will see that music means different things to different people and that it has many uses.

Think about and then discuss the following questions.

1. What role does music play in your life? Do you sing or play an instrument? Make a list of your favorite kinds of music and compare it with those of your classmates.

   _____

   _____

   _____

   _____

   _____

2. What type of traditional music does your culture have? How would you describe it? What type of instruments are used? Is it still popular today?

   _____

   _____

   _____

3. Think about the effects that music has on you. Do you listen to background music when you work or study? Have you ever noticed that music relaxes you? Does it ever energize you? In what situations?

   _____

   _____

   _____

Slow Music Soothes the Savage Appetite describes an experiment (study) carried out by researchers at Johns Hopkins Medical Institutions, Baltimore, Maryland. The purpose of the experiment was to study the effects of music on eating habits.

BEFORE YOU READ

PREREADING DISCUSSION

1. Look carefully at the title of the following article. Have you ever thought of your appetite as "savage?" Have you ever noticed that music changes the way you eat?

2. Do you like to listen to music while you eat? If so, what kinds of music do you usually listen to?

READING THE ARTICLE

Read the article one time, and then ask yourself the above questions again.

● ●

Slow Music Soothes the Savage Appetite

C L A I R E   M C I N T O S H

1   Playing slow music during dinner does more than create atmosphere; it actually encourages you to eat less. In fact, a new study suggests that the type of music you listen to while you eat may well be the key to helping you shed a few pounds or to persuade finicky kids to clean their plates.

2   Researchers at Johns Hopkins Medical Institutions recently served three meals to 90 people. The first meal was served in silence. One-third of the diners asked for second helpings and the meal took about 40 minutes to finish. Three weeks later researchers served the same people the same food while playing spirited tunes, such as "Stars and Stripes Forever" and "The Beer Barrel Polka." This time half of the diners asked for second helpings and they finished eating in only 31 minutes.

3   The final meal was served with slow, relaxing music, such as Mantovani and Percy Faith. Not only did few diners ask for seconds but most of them didn't even finish their first helpings. It also took them nearly an hour to finish their meal. "Diners tarried over their food, mashing it around, cutting it up before eating it," says study-leader Maria Simonson, director of the Health, Weight and Stress Clinic at Johns Hopkins. They also reported feeling fuller and more satisfied than they did after previous meals, even though they actually ate less. And some participants even claimed the meal tasted better.

4   Some appetite-soothing suggestions: waltzes, blues, and New Age music. To whet ailing appetites, try big-band tunes or rock-and-roll.

IDENTIFYING THE MAIN IDEA

Find the one sentence in the article that states the main idea. Write it on the lines provided.

_____

_____

ANALYZING SUPPORT FOR THE MAIN IDEA

1. How did the author support this claim?

_____

_____

2. In your own words, describe what happened in each of the steps of the experiment.

a. _____

_____

_____

b. _____

_____

_____

c. _____

_____

_____

FIGURE IT OUT

VOCABULARY IN
CONTEXT

Using contextual clues from the article, match each word or expression in column A with a word or phrase in column B.

A	B
_____ 1. to soothe	a. sick
_____ 2. to shed	b. to make you want more
_____ 3. spirited	c. to calm
_____ 4. a helping	d. enthusiastic
_____ 5. finicky	e. a serving
_____ 6. to tarry	f. picky, overly careful
_____ 7. ailing	g. another serving
_____ 8. to whet your appetite	h. to eat everything
_____ 9. to clean your plate	i. to lose
_____ 10. seconds	j. to delay

TALK IT OVER

DISCUSSION
QUESTIONS

1. According to the latest news, research has shown that listening to Mozart's music can temporarily increase your intelligence. Some scientists feel that if children, both before and after they are born, listened to more music, they would be smarter. What is your reaction to this idea?

2. Do you think this idea is worth trying? Or, do you think it goes against nature's plans?

Background music is heard every day by millions of people. We hear it in elevators, offices, stores, restaurants, factories, and even when we are on the telephone. The most well-known producer of background music is Muzak. Many people like Muzak and enjoy listening to it. Others find it annoying and criticize it for lacking expression. Muzak's purpose, however, is not to entertain us. Its real purpose is to increase our productivity, whether we are acting as consumers or workers. In **How Muzak Manipulates You**, you will read about the effects of Muzak on your behavior.

BEFORE YOU READ

PREREADING ACTIVITY

Circle the adjectives you would use to describe background music such as Muzak. Then compare your list with those of your classmates.

pretty	nice	easy-listening	calming
manipulative	dull	flat	lively
interesting	monotonous	exciting	relaxing
annoying	expressive	repetitive	cold
inviting	soothing	dead	spirited
passionate	pointless	colorful	vivid
drab	meaningful	plain	slow
dry	offensive	stimulating	tiresome

FIRST READING

This is a challenging article. Read it one time quickly for the main ideas.

How Muzak Manipulates You

A N D R E A   D O R F M A N

1   Every day millions of people in offices, supermarkets, and factories worldwide hear the sounds of Muzak. The soundtrack has been carefully engineered to direct behavior—to improve employee performance by reducing job stress, boredom, and fatigue or to control consumers' shopping habits.

2   Background music can help or hurt business, concludes Ronald Milliman, a marketing professor at Loyola University in New Orleans. "Very few stores that play music play it for any particular purpose," he says. "But walking into an environment where music is playing apparently makes a difference."

3   Milliman measured the effects of fast and slow-tempo music on a supermarket's traffic flow and sales. Fast music hardly affected sales when compared with no music, he reported in the *Journal of Marketing*, but pieces played slowly made shoppers slower and increased receipts 38 percent above what they had been when fast music was playing.

Increases Patience

4   Restaurants can also use music advantageously, he found. In the evening, slow-paced music lengthens meals and increases the patience of waiting customers. When quick turnover is important—lunch, for example—lively music does the trick.

5   The best-known supplier of background music is a company called Muzak. It was started by a group of businessmen in Cleveland, Ohio, in the early 1930s. But Muzak is not the only company of its kind. In Chicago, there is Musi-Call. In California, Musicast. And in the New York area, General Background Music (GBM).

6   Muzak calls its product "environmental music" and has done over one hundred studies—from simple surveys of employee responses to comparison of production output before and after Muzak installation—to prove its effectiveness. Improvement generally ranges from 5 to 10 percent to as much as 30 percent.

Results are easier to obtain when routine tasks are involved, but people with relatively interesting jobs are also affected.

7   The key to Muzak's programs is something called stimulus progression. What that means is that each tune is given a stimulus code based on its tempo and instrumentation. "We punch these codes into our computer, and it puts the material into fifteen-minute segments of five tunes each," music director Ralph Smith explains. "We start with a slow tune that has a low-stimulus value, and gradually build to an up-tempo, pop sound."

8   After a two-minute pause, a new segment begins on a stimulus level that's higher than the preceding ones. In this way, the day's program builds to mid-morning and mid-afternoon crescendos that are designed to give workers a needed boost.

9   "Since Muzak's main function is in the workplace, we naturally have to program against people's normal slumps," Smith notes. "Around ten-thirty, you're running down a little, but lunch is still a distance away. So, about ten-fifteen, the stimulus value for the entire segment jumps up to bring you out of the doldrums."

10 "Changing the order of things produces a different effect," says psychologist William Wokoun, chairman of Muzak's scientific advisory board. "When this so-called ascending program is played in reverse, it seems to lull people to sleep. Reaction times become slower and more variable."

11 Like Muzak, GBM focuses on the mind of the nine-to-five employee. "All day long, you have ups and downs, peaks and valleys," vice president Mel Bernstein explains. "During key periods, psychological programmers change the tempo to increase workers' adrenaline flow, which in turn increases their efficiency. The music becomes part of the surroundings. Workers no longer notice its effects on their behavior."

12 The difference between GBM and Muzak, say Bernstein, is that Muzak isn't regional: it has only one product. "But there is a very definite New York sound," he asserts, "just as there is a Midwest sound and a Los Angeles sound. And we even have rainy-day music."

IDENTIFYING MAIN IDEAS

The following is a list of main ideas from the article. Locate the paragraph that contains each idea in the list. Write the number of the paragraph on the line provided.

_____ 1. Restaurants use Muzak to affect the amount of time customers spend eating.

_____ 2. Background music can help or hurt businesses.

_____ 3. Stimulus progression is the key to Muzak's programs.

_____ 4. Muzak is designed to improve worker performance and control customers' shopping habits.

_____ 5. Studies have been conducted to show the effectiveness of Muzak.

_____ 6. General Background Music (GBM) also designs its music programs with workers in mind.

_____ 7. Slow music may cause supermarket shoppers to buy more.

_____ 8. Although Muzak is the most well-known company that supplies background music, it is not the only one.

SECOND READING

Now read the article again more carefully.

RECALLING INFORMATION

How much can you remember? Complete the paragraph with information from the article. See how much you can do without referring to the article. Then look up the rest of the answers in the article.

People shopping in a supermarket, eating in a restaurant, working in a factory, or waiting in a dentist's office all have something in common. They are _____. Every day, Muzak is heard by _____. Its purpose is to _____ and _____. Restaurants also use Muzak to _____.

Many studies have been done to _____.

Circle the letter of the phrase that best completes the statement or answers the question.

1. If a restaurant owner wants to get customers in and out quickly during lunch, what kind of music should he or she play?

   a. fast music   b. slow music   c. no music

2. At about 10:15 A.M., in a typical workplace, the stimulus value of a segment of Muzak _____.

   a. is higher than the preceding one
   b. is lower than the preceding one
   c. remains the same

3. Both Muzak and GBM _____.

   a. play the same kind of music in New York and Los Angeles
   b. focus on the mind of the nine-to-five employee
   c. have several products

4. When a typical Muzak segment is played in reverse, _____.

   a. workers become energized
   b. workers become tired
   c. workers are not affected

Below are five quotes on the subject of Muzak. In small groups, discuss each quote and your reaction to it.

1. Muzak "seems to inspire great passion for or against. Why do some hate it so? Some feel that it perverts one of life's greatest pleasures—music." (Otto Friedrich)

2. In music, "The range is enormous—opera at the top and Muzak at the bottom." (Philip Glass)

3. Muzak is "horrible stuff."[1] (Ben Shahn)

4. "Muzak is my favorite kind of music. I like anything on Muzak—it's so listenable. They should have it on MTV." (Andy Warhol)

5. Muzak is "played with an almost lunatic lack of expressiveness. This is intentional: Muzak is not there to entertain. Its purpose is primarily to increase productivity in the work place."[2] (Tony Hirsh)

If the track of a CD (compact disc) were laid out in a straight line, instead of a circle, it would be eight miles (13 km) long.

[1] The quotes in items 1, 2, and 3 are from "Trapped in a Musical Elevator," *Time* (Dec. 10, 1984).
[2] The quotes in items 4 and 5 are from "Muzak's Five Decades of Art-free Melody," *Newsweek* (Sept. 10, 1984).

Ray Charles is a popular North American singer and pianist. He was born in Albany, Georgia, in 1930 and has been blind since he was six years old. Because of his fine ear, resonant voice, and deep love for music Ray Charles has achieved great success. His style is a combination of blues, jazz, and rock and roll. In the following interview, **Ray Charles**, the singer discusses his views on music, love, and life.

BEFORE YOU READ

Look at the picture of Ray Charles that accompanies the interview. How would you describe the expression on his face? What does this picture tell you about the kind of person Ray Charles might be?

Ray Charles

Kristine Mc Kenna

W hat appeals to me, honey, is the music. I can't expect the public to come to me— I'm not that great.

Among other things, you're regarded as one of America's great masters of the blues, a musical idiom that's essentially about loss, particularly the loss of romantic love. Why does love die?

1   People often get into love affairs because they have unrealistic expectations about somebody, then when the person don't turn out to be who they thought he or she was, they start thinking maybe I can change him or her. That kind of thinking is a mistake, babe, because when the dust settles people are gonna be pretty much what they are. It's a rare thing for anybody to be able to change who they really are deep down inside and this creates a lot of problems in the romantic love department.

Do you ever make yourself cry when you sing?

2   No not at this stage—I'm an old man, darlin'. But the songs can still get through to me.

What songwriters are currently exciting you?

3   I don't know about songwriters per se. Once in a while I'll listen to the radio to see what they're putting out, but it's not too often I hear something I like. As far as rap music goes, I've been reciting poetry since I was three years old and as a musician I want the music to do something to me. Somebody like Art Tatum can make me sit up and take notice, but rap music isn't very musical and I can't learn anything from it. You gotta do something more than talk to me.

What's the most difficult kind of music to sing?

4   I know this sounds egotistical, but if I like something I can sing it. I did *Porgy and Bess*[1] and that's said to be a complicated piece of music, and I can do country music, blues and love songs. On the other hand, I can't sing something I don't like, and that's one of my defects.

Can you perform music that's out of sync with the mood you might be in on a given night?

5   Yes, because when you sing you're like an actor performing a part. Once you get out there you become that part, only you're using music instead of dialogue. I'm the kind of a person that if my personal life is hurting, I can go to work and the music will take over. It's like a guy who goes to a bar and drinks—for those few hours I can wrap myself up in my music.

Can you also be transported that way as a listener?

6   No. Listening is a different experience because when you're performing you set the mood, and when you listen the mood's already created for you. But as a listener I've loved many performers. Muddy Waters, Big Boy Crudup, Tampa Red, Nat King Cole, Al Hibler, Charles Brown, Frank Sinatra, Little Jimmy Scott—I've heard many very great performers.

At 62, you continue to spend a large percentage of your life touring. What appeals to you about life on the road?

7   What appeals to me, honey, is the music. I can't expect the public to come to me—I'm not that great. I don't especially love life on the road, but I figure if you're lucky enough to be able to do what you truly love doing and you can make a living at it, you've got the ultimate in life. Every good thing involves some kind of sacrifice, and staying in a hotel ain't too big a sacrifice in exchange for what I get from music. It can be a hassle dealing with airlines and hotels, but you have to keep reminding

---

[1] ***Porgy and Bess*** Opera composed in 1935 by George Gershwin. It is said to be the most popular opera by an American composer.

yourself: Hey, yesterday I had a beautiful day. Today isn't so hot, but as long as I keep the percentage in my favor I'm doing okay. I've accepted that I'm gonna have days where I run into nuts and people who don't know anything about nothing, and they can be in positions of authority too. But you gotta deal with them, so what can you do?

What's the most widely held misconception about the life of a famous musician?

8   That it's all glamour. People think famous people don't have the same trouble they do, but we do. Playing music don't mean life treats you any better.

How do you feel about being recognized everywhere you go?

9   You'd think I'd be used to it by now, but I still find it fascinating. You go to a little town in Japan where nobody speaks English, yet they know you on sight and know all your music. I'm not a head of state or nothing—I don't do nothing but play music—and I'm still amazed by the love people express for me and my music.

What do you think it is in your music that elicits such a strong response?

10   I hope it's the honesty. I don't lie with my music or try to bull people or feed them anything phony. I don't give them plastic. If something ain't right when I'm performing, the audience knows it because I go crazy. I'm ultra-sensitive when it comes to music, and I think the audience knows I'm genuine and that I don't give them the cheap stuff.

HOW WELL DID YOU READ?

Which of the following statements do you think Ray Charles would agree with? Circle the number of those statements.

1. It's very difficult to change someone, even if you love that person.

2. Rap is a moving and exciting type of music.

3. Liking a piece of music is an important part of being able to perform it well.

4. Listening to music and performing it are very similar kinds of experiences.

5. One of the greatest things in life is being able to make money doing what you like.

6. Famous people have fewer troubles than ordinary people.

Much of what Ray Charles says in the interview is philosophical. How would you describe his philosophy of each of the following topics?

1. Love: _____

_____

2. Music: _____

_____

3. Performance: _____

_____

4. Life: _____

_____

5. Honesty: _____

_____

FYi

John Lennon and Paul McCartney wrote the most number-one singles. By 1985, the Beatles had sold over 1 billion recordings.

VOCABULARY

INFORMAL
LANGUAGE

This is a transcript from an oral interview. You may have noticed that Ray Charles uses some language that is appropriate for speaking but that is not considered the formal written style. For example, he says "gonna," which means "going to." "Gonna" is fine if you are having a conversation, but it should be avoided in writing. He also uses street language, such as "If something ain't right," which means "If something isn't right. . . ."

Read the interview again and look for more examples of informal or street language. Make a list of them below.

_____

_____

_____

_____

Have you ever used music to make you feel better when you are sick, upset, or overtired? **Music's Surprising Power to Heal** provides evidence that music can be a powerful source of healing.

This article is long and has some technical terms you may not be familiar with. Remember that it is not necessary to understand every word you encounter. Be satisfied with a general understanding of what you read.

BEFORE YOU READ

PREREADING ACTIVITY

It will be much easier for you to understand this article if you do some work before you read it. Preview the article first, and answer the following questions.

1. Based on the title of this article, what do you think it will be about?

_____

_____

2. Skim the first and last paragraphs. Do they reinforce your prediction or make you want to change it? If you now have a new prediction, write it here.

_____

_____

3. Look at the structure of the article. You will notice that the author listed three key medical areas in italics. Make a list of these three points and think about how they might fit in with the main idea of the article.

_____

_____

READING THE ARTICLE

The author develops his ideas by using a series of anecdotes, which are short stories about a particular person or event. He also quotes many authorities in the fields of medicine and music therapy. Pay attention to these anecdotes and quotes as you read.

Music's Surprising Power to Heal

DAVID M. MAZIE

1   arianne Strebely, severely injured in an auto accident, lay in the operating room of St. Luke's Hospital in Cleveland, awaiting anesthesia. Surrounded by a surgical team, Strebely was hooked up to a computer that monitored her heart rate and brain waves. She was also hooked up, by earphones, to a tape recorder playing Vivaldi's *The Four Seasons*.

2   During the operation, the surgical team listened to Mozart and Brahms from another tape recorder. "Music reduces staff tension in the operating room," says Dr. Clyde L. Nash, Jr., Strebely's surgeon, "and also helps relax the patient."

3   "The music was better than medication," Strebely claims, comparing this surgery with a previous one. "I remained calm before the operation and didn't need as much sedation." At home, convalescing to music, Strebely was even able to forgo her prescribed painkillers.

4   Nash is one of many physicians around the country who are finding that music, used with conventional therapies, can help heal the sick. Adds Dr. Mathew H. M. Lee, acting director of the Rusk Rehabilitation Institute at New York University Medical Center, "We've seen confirmation of music's benefits in helping to avoid serious complications during illness, enhancing patients' well-being and shortening hospital stays."

5   • At California State University in Fresno, psychologist Janet Lapp studied 30 migraine-headache sufferers for five weeks. Some of the 30 listened to their favorite music; others used biofeedback and relaxation techniques; a control group did neither. All three groups received similar medication. Music proved the most effective supple-

mental therapy, especially over the long term. A year later, the patients who had continued to listen to music reported one-sixth as many headaches as before; these were also less severe and ended more quickly.

6 • At Baltimore's St. Agnes Hospital, classical music was provided in the critical-care units. "Half an hour of music produced the same effect as ten milligrams of Valium," says Dr. Raymond Bahr, head of the coronary-care unit. "Some patients who had been awake for three or four straight days were able to go into a deep sleep."

7 How does music help? Some studies show it can lower blood pressure, basal-metabolism, and respiration rates, thus lessening physiological responses to stress. Other studies suggest music may help increase production of endorphins (natural pain relievers) and S-IgA (salivary immunoglobulin A). S-IgA speeds healing, reduces the danger of infection, and controls heart rate.

8 Music therapy is proving especially effective in three key medical areas:

9 *1. Pain, anxiety, and depression.* "When I had my first baby," says Susan Koletsky of Shaker Heights, Ohio, "I was in difficult labor for two days. The second time around, I wanted to avoid the pain." Relaxing jazz calmed her in the delivery room; Bach and Beethoven paced her during contractions; finally, the closing movement of Brahms's Symphony No. 1 energized her for the last phase of delivery. "The music produced a much easier experience," she claims.

10 Cancer patients often brood in their hospital rooms, refusing to talk with doctors and nurses. "The music therapist can give them a positive outlook," says Dr. Nathan A. Berger, director of the Ireland Cancer Center at University Hospitals of Cleveland. "That makes it easier to communicate and encourages them to cooperate more in their treatment."

11 A 17-year-old patient at the center, with extensive skin damage from cancer treatments, was withdrawn and silent. When music therapist Deforia Lane saw her, the teen-ager was wrapped in gauze, sitting in a wheelchair.

12 Lane gave her a quick lesson in the omnichord, a small music synthesizer; then they played and sang together for 45 minutes. After the session, the patient's mother told Lane in a voice choked with emotion, "This is the first time Ginny has shown any happiness since she walked into this hospital."

13 *2. Mental, emotional, and physical handicaps.* The Ivymount School in Rockville, Md., helps youngsters with developmental problems ranging from emotional disturbances to mental retardation, autism, and severe to moderate learning disabilities. Ruthlee Adler, a music therapist for more than 20 years, uses song and dance to help the children learn—and cope. "While the seriously handicapped may ignore other kinds of stimulation, they respond to music," she says.

14   At Colorado State University's Center for Biomedical Research in Music, ten stroke victims were hooked up to sensors that measured muscle activity in their legs and the timing of their strides as they walked to a rhythmic dance piece. Over four weeks, the patients were tested first without, then with, the music. Significant improvement in stride symmetry was seen when the patients walked to musical accompaniment. "In almost every case," says Michael Thaut, director of the center, "the timing of the stride improved with music."

15   *3. Neurological disorders.* Dr. Oliver Sacks, whose work with sleeping-sickness victims led to the book and movie *Awakenings*, reports that patients suffering neurological disorders who cannot talk or move are often able to sing, and sometimes even dance, to music. "The power of music is remarkable in such people," Sacks observes.

16   In a group session for elderly patients at Beth Abraham Hospital in New York City, a 70-year-old stroke victim sat by himself, never speaking. One day, when therapist Connie Tomaino played an old Jewish folk song on her accordion, the man hummed. Tomaino played the tune regularly after that. Finally, the man sang some of the words. "Before you knew it," says Tomaino, "he was talking."

17   Music's therapeutic benefits, of course, aren't confined to those who are ill. "Apart from the simple enjoyment that music provides, we're learning how much it can also help us in our daily personal lives," says Ireland Cancer Center's Dr. Berger. To "psyche up" for important presentations and meetings, Berger hums the theme music from the movie *Rocky* or the triumphal march from the opera *Aïda*. "Music can also act as a tension- or pain-reliever for something as routine as going to the dentist," he says, "or it can simply give expression to our moods."

18   To gain the full benefit of music, you need to work it into your daily schedule. During his lunch hour, Jeffrey Scheffel closes his office door at the Mayo Clinic in Rochester, Minn., slips on a pair of earphones, and, leaning back in his desk chair, tunes in some light jazz or Mozart, depending on the mood he wants to build. "It rejuvenates me," explains Scheffel, research administrator at the famed medical center. "It gives my brain a break, lets me focus on something else for a few minutes, and helps me get through the rest of the day."

19   Few people understand the therapeutic powers of music better than Cleveland music therapist Deforia Lane. Ten years ago, during her own bout with cancer, singing helped her relax and take her mind off the disease. Since then, she has used that experience to help others. "Music is not magic," says the 44-year-old therapist with the warm smile and rich soprano voice. "But in a hospital or at home, for young people or older ones, it can be a potent medicine that helps us all."

SCANNING FOR DETAILS

The chart below contains some information about five of the professionals mentioned in "Music's Surprising Power to Heal." Scan the article to fill in the empty boxes in the chart.

NAME	POSITION	OPINION
		Music reduces staff tension in the operating room.
Dr. Mathew H. M. Lee		
	Music therapist	Seriously handicapped people who may ignore other kinds of stimulation respond to music.
Dr. Oliver Sacks		
	Director of the Ireland Cancer Center at University Hospitals of Cleveland	

FIGURE IT OUT

Refer to the article to answer the vocabulary questions below.

1. What phrase in paragraph 1 means "connected to"?

_____

2. What word in paragraph 3 means spending time getting well after an illness?

_____

3. Which word in paragraph 4 means something that adds new difficulties?

_____

4. Which word in paragraph 6 means "consecutive"?

_____

(continued on the next page)

5. Which word in paragraph 10 means to think about one's troubles?

_____

6. What word in paragraph 12 is a kind of small musical instrument?

_____

7. Which word in paragraph 13 is the opposite of "to pay attention"?

_____

8. Which word in paragraph 15 is used to describe something that is out of the ordinary?

_____

9. Which word in paragraph 17 means "regular" or "ordinary"?

_____

10. Which word in paragraph 18 means "well-known"?

_____

HOW WELL DID YOU READ?

1. Studies show several ways that music can help patients. Make a list of some of these ways.

_____   _____

2. According to the author, music can also help people who are not sick. What are some of the ways music can help people in their daily lives?

3. The article ends with a quote by music therapist and cancer patient Deforia Lane. She says, "Music is not magic. But in a hospital or at home, for young people or older ones, it can be a potent medicine that helps us all." Find specific evidence in the article to support her belief.

_____

TALK IT OVER

DISCUSSION QUESTIONS

1. Have you had any personal experiences with the healing power of music?

2. Why do you think music can be a powerful source of healing?

PALINDROMES,
OXYMORONS,
PLEONASMS,
HOMONYMS

PALINDROMES

A. Look at the following list of words and phrases. Do you notice anything unusual about them?

noon	refer	live not on evil
mom	sees	Norma, I am Ron
Otto	race car	no melon, no lemon
wow		

B. Based on your observations, write a definition of a palindrome.

_____

C. What other palindromes can you think of?

_____

According to the *Guinness Book of World Records*, the longest single-word English palindrome is "tattarattat" which means the sound of someone knocking at the door.

OXYMORONS

When two words that seem to be opposites or contradictory are used together, we call them an oxymoron.

Read and think about the following oxymorons[1] so that you understand them, and then try to write some of your own.

plastic glasses	almost perfect	routine emergency
poor little rich girl	small crowd	full-time hobby
clearly confused		

_____   _____

PLEONASMS

Two words that are redundant when they are used together are called pleonasms. We use pleonasms every day without even realizing it.

Read the following pleonasms[2] and then think of some more on your own.

blue sky	sharp point	exciting adventure
frozen ice	round circle	hot fire

_____   _____

1 From *Pretty Ugly,* by Warren Blumenfeld (New York: Putnam, 1989).
2 Ibid.

165

Look at the following list of words and phrases and try to decide which ones are palindromes, oxymorons, and pleonasms. Write *Pal* next to the palindromes, *Oxy* next to the oxymorons, and *Ple* next to the pleonasms. Then check your answers in the Answer Key on page 213.

1. _____ sandy beaches

2. _____ level

3. _____ science fiction

4. _____ live evil

5. _____ radar

6. _____ good loser

7. _____ equal halves

8. _____ stop spots

9. _____ Hannah

10. _____ talk show

11. _____ madam I'm Adam

12. _____ make haste slowly

13. _____ a Toyota

14. _____ healthy junk food

15. _____ almost totally

16. _____ original copy

17. _____ student teacher

18. _____ my gym

19. _____ nondairy creamer

20. _____ real magic

21. _____ whole life

22. _____ low-calorie sweetener

23. _____ leisure suit

24. _____ too hot to hoot

25. _____ fake fur

26. _____ routine emergency

HOMONYMS

Homonyms are words that sound alike but are spelled differently and have different meanings. For example, *to* and *two* are homonyms. They are pronounced the same, but one means *also* and the other is the number that follows *one*. Also, they are spelled differently.

Try to figure out a pair of homonyms for each of the following clues. Then check your answers in the Answer Key on page 213.

1. something that you swim in, and what you do with your eyes:

_____   _____

2. to escape, and an insect that lives on cats and dogs:

_____   _____

3. a color, and what you did with a book:

_____   _____

4. part of your foot, and to pull something:

_____   _____

5. a color, and what the wind did:

_____   _____

6. something you did with a baseball, and a word meaning finished:

_____   _____

7. how heavy you are, and to anticipate:

_____   _____

POSTREADING DISCUSSION QUESTIONS

1. Read the following quotations and discuss what their authors meant. Then discuss your reactions to the quotes.

   a. "Of all the noises, I think music is the least disagreeable."[1] (Samuel Johnson)

   b. "Music is more a physical and direct kind of high than art. The satisfaction is the same, but while doing it [the music], it is more immediate; art is far more intellectual." (Rickie Lee)

   c. "I'm addicted to music. For me it's not an entirely healthy kind of drug because the music I like makes me sad. It moves me in a way that art rarely does."[2] (Jim Shaw)

2. How do you feel about the use of music to manipulate people?

3. What composers and music move you? Why? In what ways?

4. What other benefits of music can you think of?

READER'S JOURNAL

Write for ten to twenty minutes in your Reader's Journal on the subject of music. Use information from the articles or your personal thoughts and experiences to write about your feelings toward music.

[1]Samuel Johnson, in the *Book of Humorous Quotations,* edited by A. S. Adams (New York: Dodd, Mead and Co., 1969).
[2]The quotes in items 2 and 3 are from *Art News* (October 1992), p. 18.

READER'S JOURNAL

Date: _____

ARE YOU SUPERSTITIOUS?

Selections

Today we live in an age of advanced technology and science. It seems that we have an almost endless supply of scientific information at our fingertips. However, we still seem to hold on to superstitions as a way of explaining and dealing with the unknown. In this sense, we have advanced very little since prehistoric times. In this unit, you will read about the origins of some popular superstitions.

POINTS TO PONDER

DISCUSSION QUESTIONS

Think about and then discuss the following questions.

1. Are you a superstitious person? If so which, superstitions do you believe in? What purpose do they serve for you?

2. Do you think it is rational or irrational to believe in superstitions? What are people looking for in superstitions? Why do so many people act as though there were truth in superstitions?

3. Every culture has its own set of superstitions. Although some cultures share several superstitions, it is interesting to notice the differences. Make a list of some of the common superstitions in your country and compare them with those of your classmates.

_____   _____

_____   _____

_____   _____

_____

BEFORE YOU READ

PREREADING ACTIVITY

A. Look at the following photographs. Match the picture with the correct caption.

2. _____

1. _____

3. _____

4. _____

a. Walking under a ladder brings bad luck.
b. Don't open an umbrella indoors.
c. Make a wish and cross your fingers.
d. Protect yourself! Knock on wood.

B. The following article is taken from the *World Book Encyclopedia.* Before you read the article (pages 172–175), look at the subheadings and the first sentence of each paragraph. On the lines provided, make a list of the topics you think will be discussed in the article. After you have finished reading the whole article, check to see how accurate your predictions were.

_____

_____

_____

_____

_____

FIRST READING

SKIMMING

Skim each part of the article quickly without using a dictionary. Do not worry about specific details since you are only reading for the main ideas. Underline anything that seems important as you read. When you finish each part, answer the questions that follow.

● ●

Superstitions

1 **Superstition** is a traditional belief that a certain action or event can cause or foretell an apparently unrelated event. For example, some superstitious people believe that carrying a rabbit's foot will bring them good luck. Others believe that if a black cat crosses their path, they will have bad luck. To yet other superstitious people, dropping a knife or fork on the floor means company is coming. Such beliefs are superstitions because in each case the action and the event it foretells are traditionally thought to be connected. For instance, the rabbit's foot is associated with fertility.

2 Superstitions have existed in every human society throughout history. Most people, including highly educated individuals, act superstitiously from time to time. Many persons may joke about avoiding bad luck by knocking on wood or not walking under a ladder. But they have such beliefs anyway. Scholars once believed that all superstitions dated back to humanity's early history. But many superstitions have appeared in relatively recent times. According to a superstition in baseball, for example, a pitcher will give up a hit if anyone mentions that a no-hit game is being pitched.

3 Countless human activities are involved in superstitions. They include eating, sleeping, working, playing, getting married, having a baby, becoming ill, and dying. Times of danger and uncertainty have brought many superstitions. Superstitions concern animals, clothing, lakes, mountains, names, numbers, the planets and stars, the weather, and parts of the body.

HOW WELL DID YOU READ?

Put a check mark (✓) next to the statements that are true.

_____ 1. A superstition is a belief that a certain action can cause another unrelated action.

_____ 2. Only a few societies throughout history have had superstitions.

_____ 3. Although scholars used to think all superstitions were very old, many of them are relatively new.

_____ 4. There are superstitions about almost every aspect of life.

4   **Kinds of superstitions**. Many superstitions deal with important events in a person's life, such as birth, entering adulthood, marriage, pregnancy, and death. Such superstitions supposedly ensure that a person will pass safely from one stage of life to the next. For example, a person born on Sunday will always have good luck. A bride and groom will have bad luck if they see each other on their wedding day before the ceremony. A pregnant woman must eat the right food, or she will give her child an unwanted birthmark. After a person dies, the doors and windows of the room should be opened so the spirit can leave.

5   Some superstitions involve a type of magic. One form of such magic comes from the belief that similar actions produce similar results. Many people believe a newborn baby must be carried upstairs before being carried downstairs. In this way, the child will be assured of rising in the world and having success. The same principle appears in the custom of putting money in a purse or wallet being given as a gift. The giver wants to make sure the purse or wallet will always contain money.

6   A number of superstitions involve someone's taking a deliberate action to cause something to happen or to prevent something from occurring. Most of these _causal_ superstitions involve ensuring good luck, avoiding bad luck, or making something good happen. For example, carrying a silver dollar supposedly brings good luck. Some people will not start a trip on a Friday, especially if it is the 13th day of the month. Friday and the number 13 are both associated with bad luck. According to a Japanese belief, the number 4 is unlucky. This is because _shi_, the Japanese word for that number, sounds like the Japanese word that means _death_. As a result, many buildings in Japan have no fourth floor. According to another superstition, wedding guests throw rice at the newlyweds to ensure that

the marriage will result in many children. Causal superstitions may involve actions intended to give bad luck to someone. Witches supposedly perform some of these actions.

7   Other superstitions foretell an event without any conscious action by the person involved. Some of these sign superstitions foretell good or bad luck. For example, finding a horseshoe or a four-leaf clover means good luck. Breaking a mirror or spilling salt brings bad luck. Other sign superstitions foretell a certain event or condition. A ring around the moon means rain will soon fall. A howling dog means death is near. A person with red hair has a quick temper.

8   Some sign superstitions may be changed into causal superstitions. If a person hangs a horseshoe over a door, witches cannot enter. If a young woman pins a four-leaf clover to her door, she will marry the first bachelor who comes in the door. In some cases, a person may avoid the bad luck involved in a sign superstition by taking immediate action. For example, someone who has spilled salt may cancel the bad luck by throwing a pinch of salt over the left shoulder.

HOW WELL DID YOU READ?

Circle the letter of the word or phrase that best completes each statement.

1. Superstitions may involve _____.

   a. magic
   b. important events in a person's life
   c. taking an action to cause or prevent something else
   d. *(all of the above)*

2. All of the following are causal superstitions except _____.

   a. carrying a silver dollar to bring good luck
   b. finding a four-leaf clover means good luck
   c. throwing rice at newlyweds so they will have lots of children
   d. not starting a trip on Friday to avoid bad luck

3. Sign superstitions _____.

   a. cannot be changed into causal superstitions
   b. are very rare
   c. do not involve deliberate action by the person involved
   d. deal with important events in a person's life

9   **The role of superstitions**. Many people scoff at superstitions because they consider such beliefs to be unscientific. However, many scholars believe that some superstitions have a scientific basis. For example, people in England once used tea made from foxglove plants to treat some forms of heart disease. Today, physicians often prescribe digitalis, a drug made from dried leaves of the purple foxglove, for patients with weak hearts.

10   Some superstitions have a practical origin. For example, many people believe that lighting cigarettes for three individuals from one match will bring bad luck. This superstition may have originated among soldiers during World War I (1914–1918). At night, a match that stayed lit long enough to light three cigarettes provided a target for the enemy. Another superstition involves hanging a bag of garlic around a child's neck for protection from illness. The garlic-filled bag has no supernatural power. But its smell keeps away other children—including any who have a disease that the wearer of the bag might catch.

11   Most people have fears that make them insecure. Superstitions help overcome such fears by providing security. They reassure people that they will get what they want and avoid trouble. For example, millions of people believe in astrology and base important decisions on the position of the sun, moon, planets, and stars. Superstitions will probably have a part in life as long as people fear each other and have uncertainties about the future.

● ●

HOW WELL DID YOU READ?

Complete each sentence with one word to make the statement true.

1. Some people laugh at superstitions because they think superstitions are _____.

2. Some superstitions have _____ origins.

3. Superstitions may help people deal with their fears by making them feel more _____.

4. _____ will probably be a part of life for a long time.

Now read the article again more carefully, paying special attention to the organization.

An **outline** is an organized analysis of a reading selection. It is often used to help students see the organizational patterns of a reading. Making your own outline of an article will help you understand its basic structure. It will also clarify the relationships between main and supporting ideas.

In the following outline of "Superstition," Roman numerals introduce the general topics, capital letters are used to indicate main ideas, and numbers are used for supporting information. Most of the main ideas in this article are stated in the topic sentence of each paragraph. The main ideas are then supported with specific examples.

Complete the outline.

I. Background Information

    A. Superstition—traditional belief that a certain action or event can cause or foretell an apparently unrelated event.

        1. Carrying a rabbit's foot brings good luck.

        2. _____

        3. _____

    B. _____

       _____

        1. Scholars used to think that all superstitions were very old.

        2. _____

II. Kinds of superstitions

    A. _____

    B. These superstitions ensure that a person will pass safely from one stage of life to the next.

        1. _____

        2. _____

3. _____

4. _____

C._____

    1. _____

    2. _____

    3. Putting money in a wallet before giving it as a gift ensures it will always contain money.

D. Causal superstitions

    1. _____

    2. _____

    3. _____

E. Sign superstitions

    1. _____

    2. _____

    3. _____

    4. _____

    5. _____

DISTINGUISHING FACT FROM OPINION

Read each statement below. If you think a statement is a fact (something that can be proven), write *FC* on the line. If you think it is an opinion (someone's idea), write *OP*.

_____ 1. Doctors often give patients with weak hearts a drug called digitalis.

_____ 2. Similar actions produce similar results.

_____ 3. Throughout history, every society has had some forms of superstition.

(continued on the next page)

_____ 4. Some superstitions have a scientific basis.

_____ 5. Superstitions will be a part of life as long as people fear each other and the future.

_____ 6. Not all superstitions date back to man's early history.

APPLICATION OF INFORMATION

How superstitious are you? Answer the following questions.

1. If you break a mirror, do you think it brings seven years of bad luck? _____

2. Would you leave for a vacation on Friday the 13th? _____

3. Would you open an umbrella indoors? _____

4. Do you avoid walking under ladders? _____

5. Do you cross your fingers for good luck? _____

6. Do you avoid stepping on cracks? _____

7. Do you believe finding a four-leaf clover is good luck? _____

8. If a black cat crosses your path, do you get upset? _____

9. Do you carry a rabbit's foot for good luck? _____

10. Do you knock on wood to protect yourself against bad luck? _____

11. Do you make a wish if you see a shooting star? _____

12. Do you always enter and leave a house by the same door? _____

13. Do you believe that spilling salt brings bad luck? _____

FYi

The U. S. Treasury Department stopped printing two-dollar bills because many people considered them unlucky and refused to use them.

As you will discover in **Knock on Wood**, superstitions about sports are widespread, and athletes are one of the most superstitious groups of people.

BEFORE YOU READ

DISCUSSION

Before you read the following article, discuss any superstitions you have heard of that relate to sports. Are there any famous athletes in your country who are known for being superstitious?

● ●

Knock on Wood

Walter Roessing

1   When the Oakland Athletics[1] are on a winning streak, Manager Tony La Russa won't take off his jacket—even if the temperature is 100 degrees. Golfer Lanny Wadkins never tees off without his 1878 dollar.

2   Why? Because those men are superstitious. They believe sticking with a routine will help them win. Race car driver Mario Andretti won't enter a car from the right side or stay in a hotel room with the number 13. Ronnie Lott of the Los Angeles Raiders always wears his lucky swim shorts under his football uniform.

3   "Athletes are more superstitious than most people," Lott says. "They do all kinds of crazy things to guarantee victory or make sure they won't get hurt. The one time I forgot to wear my lucky plaid Hawaiian shorts for a game, I dislocated my shoulder."

4   But Lott isn't as superstitious as some baseball stars were long ago. They practiced odd rituals with their

[1] Oakland Athletics A baseball team located in Oakland, California.

bats in order to "guarantee" hits.

5   Richie Ashburn, who played in the 1950s, slept with his bats on road trips. Hall of Famer Eddie Collins, who played from 1906 to 1930, buried his bats in the ground to keep them lively.

6   "Whatever the superstitions, they help athletes and coaches relax," says sports psychologist Thomas Tutko of San Jose State University in California.

7   Superstitious beliefs often involve food, numbers, or rituals.

8   **Food:** Dedicated baseball fans know that Boston's Wade Boggs eats chicken before every game. That quirk started when Boggs was in the minor leagues. "On those days when I ate chicken, I always got two hits," he says.

9   Lott always eats a hamburger the night before a game. Several years ago, his team was playing away on Thanksgiving Day. The night before, Lott passed up a turkey dinner with his teammates to dine alone at Wendy's.

10   **Numbers:** Boggs is hung up on the numbers 7 and 17. Before a night game, he always runs in the outfield at exactly 7:17 P.M.

11   **Rituals:** Tutko, the psychologist, recalls working with San Jose-area high school basketball players who believed they were winning because of their white socks.

12   "They refused to wash their socks all season," Tutko says. "By the last game, their socks were standing straighter than their shoes."

13   Golfer Mark Calcavecchia figures he won more than $330,000 on the pro tour by wearing his lucky golf outfit: beige slacks and a beige-and-brown shirt.

14   "My wife thought it was ugly," he admits. "But before I retired it, I won two events and finished second in another."

15   Mark van Eeghen was a star fullback for the Oakland Raiders. Before each game, he would climb atop the television set in his hotel room and leap to the bed. He felt that was insurance against getting hurt on the field. But one time, he missed the bed. His injury forced him to miss one game.

16   Some rituals can be downright weird. Here is an example: In the 1988 National League pennant race, San Diego was a thorn in Houston's side. The Astros had lost 11 straight games at San Diego. So Houston pitcher Jim Deshaies took matters into his own hands.

17   He bought a book on how to break curses. Then he entered Houston's clubhouse with branches from four trees.

18   First he broke the branches. Then he spit on them. Next, he set them on fire and chanted some words. The result? Houston defeated San Diego, 4–1.

19   It seems some athletes will do anything for good luck.

SCANNING FOR DETAILS

Complete the chart with information from the article.

Athlete	Sport	Superstitions
Richie Ashburn		
		eats chicken before every game; runs in out-field at exactly 7:17 P.M. every day
	race car driver	
Tony La Russa		
	star fullback for Oakland Raiders	
		wears lucky swim shorts under his football uniform; always eats hamburger before game
	golfer	
Lanny Wadkins		

HOW WELL DID YOU READ?

1. Why do some athletes believe in superstitions?

2. According to sports psychologist Thomas Tutko, what is the benefit of superstitions?

3. What three areas do superstitious beliefs often involve?

4. According to the author, baseball stars used to be even more superstitious than they are today. What two examples does he give to support his claim?

Many superstitions involve the belief in lucky and unlucky numbers. **What Will Tomorrow Bring?** discusses some of these numbers and the origins of the superstitions involving them.

1. Many people are superstitious when it comes to choosing a lucky number. Do you have any lucky numbers that you depend on? What are they?

2. How did you choose your lucky numbers and what significance do they have? When do you use them?

● ●

What Will Tomorrow Bring?

D A N I E L   C O H E N

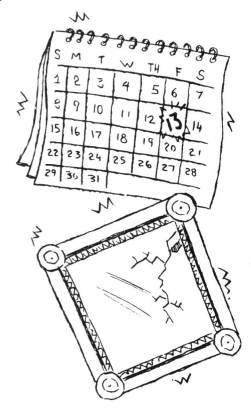

1   The next time you ride an elevator in a tall building see if there is a 13th floor. Some buildings have one, but others do not. From the 12th floor, they skip right to the 14th. What happened to the 13th floor? It is there, of course, but it is called 14. In this and similar situations, the number 13 is frequently avoided. The "Devil's dozen"—an old name for 13—is supposed to bring bad luck.

2   There is nothing lucky or unlucky about any number. The belief that a number can bring good or bad luck is a superstition held by a surpris-

ingly large number of people. A superstition is a belief or practice that does not rely on fact but is usually based on fear of the unknown or on ignorance. Most superstitions are supposed to make something good happen or prevent misfortune.

The 13th Guest

3   The 13th day of the month, particularly if it is a Friday, is regarded as unlucky by superstitious people. Many of us joke about Friday the 13th. But others are cautious about their activities on that day for fear that an accident or other disaster may occur. Some superstitious people also consider it unlucky for a group of 13 to eat dinner together. One of them, according to the superstition, will die within a year.

4   We do not know how the number 13 got its bad reputation. "Unlucky 13" may have started with the Vikings or other Norsemen. They told the story of a great banquet for 12 guests—all of them gods. The evil god Loki, angry at not being invited, sneaked into the banquet. Now there were 13 guests. One of the gods at the banquet was killed, and since that time—the story goes—the number 13 has been considered unlucky.

5   Some think the belief started with Christianity. At the Last Supper, there were 13—Jesus Christ and the 12 apostles. The Last Supper was followed by Christ's crucifixion so that, again, the number 13 was identified with a dreadful event. It is believed that Christ was crucified on a Friday. This explains why Friday is regarded by some superstitious people as unlucky. For example, Friday is supposed to be a bad day to start a new job, to begin a voyage, to cut one's nails, or to get married.

Your Own Image

6   "Breaking a mirror brings 7 years' bad luck," goes the old superstition. Of course, it is dangerous to break anything made of glass because you may cut your hand. But there are no superstitious beliefs attached to breaking a drinking glass or a light bulb. The mirror is special because you can see your own image in it.

7   The mirror belief began thousands of years ago, when man thought that his image (picture, sculpture, or reflection) was part of him. He believed, too, that what happened to his image would happen to him.

8   The first mirrors were probably quiet ponds. When a man looked into a pond and saw his image, smooth and unruffled, it was a sign that the gods would be good to him. But if the image was broken and distorted by ripples, there was trouble ahead.

9　Mirror images are clear unless the mirror is cracked. Originally, the image itself was thought to foretell the future. As time passed, the cracked mirror rather than the image became the sign of bad luck.

3 Plus 4

10　Why is a cracked mirror supposed to cause 7 years' bad luck? Seven is a special number that for thousands of years has meant either good or bad luck. Its supposed magic dates back to early superstitious beliefs about the numbers 3 and 4. Once numbers were more than signs for counting all sorts of quantities. They also represented specific things or ideas.

11　Today we generally do not identify the number 3 with anything in particular; it is used to count books, fruit, bicycles, and so on. But to some ancient peoples, like the Egyptians, the number 3 represented the Mother, Father, and Son. These 3, called a trinity, were regarded as the basis for continuing life from one generation to the next.

12　In time, the number 3 came to represent something more than the continuation of life. Since life was mysterious and spiritual, the number 3 grew to mean the spirit or mind of man.

13　The number 4 represented the 4 chief directions—north, south, east, and west. Earth was then believed to be square. The number 4 and the 4 directions it represented were shown as a small square that looked like a house.

14　Three and 4 were combined to produce the sacred number 7. Small wonder that 7 is connected with so many superstitions! It once stood for an immensely powerful idea: the house that contains the spirit of man.

One out of eight North Americans thinks that Elvis Presley is still alive.

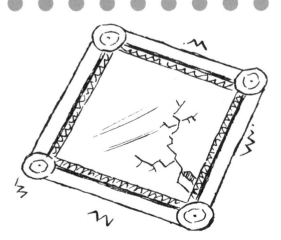

HOW WELL DID YOU READ?

Read the following statements. If a statement is true, write *T* on the line. If it is false, write *F*.

_____ 1. There are several theories about how 13 became an unlucky number.

_____ 2. The number 13 was once called the Devil's dozen.

_____ 3. Superstitions are based on scientific facts.

_____ 4. Starting a new job on a Friday could be a problem for some people who are superstitious.

_____ 5. Some superstitious people would not want to eat dinner with twelve other guests.

_____ 6. The superstition that breaking a mirror brings bad luck is very old.

_____ 7. Seven has been a special number for thousands of years and always means good luck.

_____ 8. Numbers used to mean more than they do today.

_____ 9. For some ancient peoples the number 3 had a special significance.

RECALLING INFORMATION

How much can you remember? Complete the paragraph with information from the article. See how much you can do without referring to the article. Then go back and look up the rest of the answers.

Many people are superstitious about _____. For

example, the number _____ is supposed to bring

_____ luck. We do not know exactly how it got its

bad _____. There are many theories. Some think it

may have started with the Vikings. Others think the belief

began with _____. _____ is

another number that is associated with superstitions. If you break a

_____ it is supposed to cause

(continued on the next page)

_____ of _____. Ideas about

the magic of the number _____ are very old, dating

back to superstitions about the numbers _____ and

_____. In the past, numbers were more than

_____. They represented _____.

For instance, the number three meant _____ and

the number four represented _____.

TALK IT OVER

DISCUSSION
QUESTIONS

1. Summarize the way superstitions about the following numbers may
   have started.

   13 _____

   _____

   3 _____

   _____

   4 _____

   _____

2. Discuss the origins of the superstition that breaking a mirror brings
   seven years of bad luck.

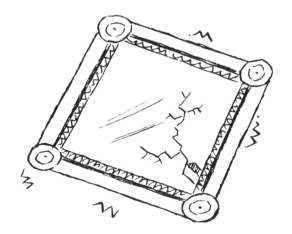

An object or a person that supposedly brings bad luck is said to be cursed or jinxed. People who believe in this superstition think that a person, place, object, or even an idea can be jinxed. In **It's Jinxed!**, you will read about a place that was supposed to be jinxed.

It's Jinxed!

D A N I E L   C O H E N

[1] Certain objects are supposed to bring good luck, but others have a reputation of being jinxed—that is, of bringing bad luck. The Hope diamond, one of the world's greatest gems, is supposed to bring misfortune to its owners. Today, this jinxed stone is on display in the Smithsonian Institution in Washington, D.C. Its reputation for bad luck does not keep thousands of visitors from flocking to see it every year.

[2] Places as well as objects can be jinxed. For example, consider the story of the "Pharaoh's Curse." The rulers, or kings, of ancient Egypt were called pharaohs. In 1922, archaeologists (scientists who study ancient civilizations) made a spectacular discovery in Egypt. They uncovered the tomb of the Pharaoh Tutankhamen, an event that made headlines throughout the world.

[3] Shortly after the tomb was opened, three people who had been connected with the expedition died. They all died of different causes, and their deaths were entirely natural. But the coincidence unleashed a flood of stories that the tomb had been cursed.

[4] There was a tale that the inscription "Death to those who enter this tomb" was carved above the tomb door. This inscription never existed. Nor did those

who believed in the curse ever bother to explain how dozens of others connected with the expedition lived long and successful lives after entering the tomb. The story of the "Pharaoh's Curse" was kept alive in newspapers and magazines for years. In the end, it proved to be one of the biggest hoaxes in the history of superstition.

Invention of a Superstition

5   Howard Carter and Lord Carnarvon became world famous in 1922 for finding the tomb of the Pharaoh Tutankhamen. When Lord Carnarvon died some months later, the "Pharaoh's Curse" was blamed.

6   The curse was mysterious and awesome—and a fraud. It was invented by reporters who wanted to provide their readers with an exciting story that would continue to sell newspapers and magazines.

7   Like many members of the expedition, Howard Carter—the chief discoverer of the tomb—lived a normal life span. He died in 1939 at the age of 66.

● ●

HOW WELL DID YOU READ?

Read the following statements. If a statement is true, write *T* on the line. If it is false, write *F*.

_____ 1. Since the Hope diamond is supposed to be jinxed, few people want to get near it.

_____ 2. Both places and objects can have reputations for being jinxed.

_____ 3. When the tomb of Pharaoh Tutankhamen was discovered, it was written about in newspapers all over the world.

_____ 4. Three people died from supernatural causes right after the tomb was opened.

_____ 5. "Death to those who enter this tomb" is written above the door of Pharaoh Tutankhamen's tomb.

_____ 6. "The Pharaoh's Curse" is one of the biggest hoaxes in the history of superstitions.

FIGURE IT OUT

VOCABULARY IN CONTEXT

Without using your dictionary, write an approximate definition or a synonym for the highlighted words in the following sentences.

1. *Certain objects are supposed to bring good luck, but others have a reputation of being **jinxed**—that is, of bringing bad luck.*

2. *Its reputation for bad luck does not keep thousands of visitors from **flocking** to see it every year.*

_____

3. *In 1922, **archaeologists** (scientists who study ancient civilizations) made a spectacular discovery in Egypt.*

_____

4. *There was a tale that the **inscription** "Death to those who enter this tomb" was carved above the tomb door.*

_____

5. *The curse was mysterious and awesome—and a **fraud**. It was invented by reporters who wanted to provide their readers with an exciting story. . . .*

_____

6. *The rulers, or kings, of ancient Egypt were called **pharaohs**.*

_____

IDENTIFYING MAIN IDEAS

The following is a list of main ideas from the article. Locate the paragraph that contains each idea on the list. Write the number of the paragraph on the line provided.

_____ 1. Objects such as the Hope diamond have a reputation of being jinxed.

_____ 2. By coincidence, three people connected with the expedition of Pharaoh Tutankhamen's tomb died.

_____ 3. The story of the "Pharaoh's Curse" proved to be a hoax.

_____ 4. Places like Pharaoh Tutankhamen's tomb can also be jinxed.

APPLICATION OF INFORMATION

Imagine that you were a reporter in 1922. Write a story for your newspaper reporting the discovery of the pharaoh's tomb and the mysterious death of Howard Carter. Be sure to include a headline that would catch your readers' attention.

Below you will see a list of questions. Each one refers to a superstition mentioned in this unit. Write the correct answer in the spaces below. The last letter of an answer will always be the first letter of the next answer. Then check your answers in the Answer Key on page 213.

Examples:

What bird causes bad luck if it flies into your house?

<u>r</u> <u>o</u> <u>b</u> <u>i</u> <u>n</u>

For good luck, rice is thrown at what couple?

<u>n</u> <u>e</u> <u>w</u> <u>l</u> <u>y</u> <u>w</u> <u>e</u> <u>d</u>

1. What brings bad luck if you open it indoors?

—— —————————

2. What should you do when you're taking a walk?

————— <u>l</u> <u>a</u> <u>d</u> <u>d</u> <u>e</u> <u>r</u> <u>s</u>

3. What shouldn't you do when you're walking on a sidewalk?

———— —— —————

4. What brings bad luck if you do it at the table?

————— ————

5. What is an unlucky number?

———————

6. What do robins build that bring good luck in the spring?

————

7. What can you wish on?

<u>a</u> —————— ————

8. What is something that you can carry for good luck?

a __ __ __ __ __ __'s __ __ __ __

9. What place is thought to be jinxed?

__ __ __ __ __ __ __ __ __ __ __ __'s __ __ __ __

10. What brings seven years of bad luck?

__ __ __ __ __ __ __ __ a __ __ __ __ __ __

POSTREADING DISCUSSION QUESTIONS

1. For thousands of years people have believed in superstitions. Why? What are we looking for when we accept superstitions?

2. Something that is "paranormal" is difficult to explain. The paranormal includes belief in superstitions, astrology, magic, faith healers, witchcraft, and others. Do you feel that it is dangerous for people to believe in the paranormal? Why or why not?

3. Do you think that believing in superstitions is unscientific? Do you believe that science can find a satisfactory explanation for everything? Why or why not? Give specific examples to support your answer.

4. Humorist and journalist Don Marquis has observed that "Science has always been too dignified to invent a good back-scratcher." What does this quote mean? Do you agree or disagree with it? What does the quote mean in terms of the debate between science and superstition?

READER'S JOURNAL

Write for ten to twenty minutes in your Reader's Journal about your thoughts on superstitions. Be as specific as you can and give lots of examples to support your ideas.

READER'S JOURNAL

Date: _____

_____

_____

_____

_____

_____

_____

_____

_____

_____

_____

_____

_____

_____

_____

_____

_____

_____

_____

_____

OUR SHRINKING WORLD

FYi
Unit·8

Selections

In the past, each individual country had its own separate and distinct cultural identity. This is no longer completely true. Technological advances in communication, transportation, politics, and business have increased the cultural interactions among countries and culture groups to the point that very few cultures are now completely isolated. This process of breaking down national barriers, known as globalization, is changing the world as we know it. In this unit you will read about some of the forces at work in making our world seem smaller and smaller.

Think about and then discuss the following questions.

1. Think about ways that globalization has caused your life to be different from the lives of your parents when they were your age. Make a list of at least three ways and share your ideas with your classmates.

_____

_____

_____

2. Think about ways you think the world might be different for your children or grandchildren.

_____

_____

_____

3. It is often said that the world is shrinking. Do you think this is a natural result of the world's increasing population? Why or why not?

_____

_____

_____

As the world grows smaller, the value of bi- or multilingualism increases. People who master a foreign language have more opportunities for work and advancement. **Jobs in a Shrinking World** is taken from a book about career opportunities for Americans who speak foreign languages. It discusses the many career advantages of multilingualism.

BEFORE YOU READ

PREREADING ACTIVITIES

1. **Before you read this selection, think about the following quote taken from the same book:**

Fluency in a foreign language is not only possible; it's increasingly beneficial. The world keeps getting smaller. It used to take a week bouncing around on the Atlantic Ocean to get from New York to Paris. Nowadays, an airplane will get you there in a few hours. Since it is so easy to travel now, many more people are doing it. Business people, students, tourists—they all crowd the roads, railways, and airways. Increased travel means greater opportunity and incentive to learn foreign languages.[1]

Write a few sentences about what you think this quote means.

_____

_____

_____

_____

_____

_____

_____

2. **The first paragraph in the selection mentions the term** *global village.* **Discuss the meaning of this expression with your classmates.**

[1] From H. Ned Seelye, J. Laurence Day, *VGM Career Horizons: Careers for Language Aficionados and other Multi-lingual Types.*

Jobs in a Shrinking World

H. NED SEELYE, J. LAURENCE DAY

1   New technology links the world as never before. Our planet has
shrunk. It's now a "global village" where countries are only seconds away by fax or phone or satellite link. Teleconferencing,
portable satellite links, radio telephones, and other high-tech
advances make foreign markets as close as our crosstown branch
office. And, of course, our ability to benefit from this high-tech
communication equipment is greatly enhanced by foreign language skills.

2   Deeply involved with this new technology is a breed of modern businesspeople who have a growing respect for the economic value of doing business abroad. In modern markets, success overseas often helps support and revitalize domestic business efforts.

3   Overseas assignments are becoming increasingly important to advancement within executive ranks. The executive stationed in another country no longer need fear being "out of sight and out of mind." He or she can be sure that the overseas effort is central to the company's plan for success, and that promotions often follow or accompany an assignment abroad. If an employee can succeed in a difficult assignment overseas, superiors will have greater confidence in his or her ability to cope back in the United States where cross-cultural considerations and foreign language issues are becoming more and more prevalent.

4   Thanks to a variety of relatively inexpensive communications devices with business applications, even small businesses in the United States are able to get into markets where the medium of exchange is the mark, the yen, the peso, or the pound. Large corporations have international branches or divisions, and they deal with foreign investors and buyers on a daily basis.

5   English is still the international language of business. The American dollar still talks clearly in the world marketplace. But there is an ever-growing need for people who can decipher another tongue. A second language isn't generally required to get a job in business, but having language skills gives a candidate the edge when other qualifications appear to be equal.

6   The employee posted abroad who speaks the country's principal language has an opportunity to fast-forward certain negotiations, and can have the cultural insight to know when it is better to move more slowly. The employee at the home office who can communicate well with foreign clients over the telephone or by fax machine is an obvious asset to the firm. Such persons build a niche for themselves in the firm. They find themselves included in the "loop" in which key company business is discussed.

● ●

IDENTIFYING THE MAIN IDEA   **In your own words, write one sentence that reflects the main idea of the whole selection.**

**DISTINGUISHING
MAIN IDEAS
FROM
SUPPORTING
POINTS**

The following is a list of ideas taken from the text. Write *M* next to
those statements you think are main ideas and *S* next to the ones you
think are supporting details.

_____ 1. New technology links the world as never before.

_____ 2. Teleconferences, portable satellites, and radio telephones make
foreign markets very close.

_____ 3. Promotion often follows an assignment in another country.

_____ 4. Even small businesses in the U.S. are getting into the foreign
market.

_____ 5. A second language isn't required to get a job in business, but it
helps.

_____ 6. An employee working in another country who speaks the
native language can influence negotiations.

_____ 7. The ability to communicate with foreign clients over the
phone is an asset.

_____ 8. Modern businesspeople are increasingly aware of the economic benefits of doing business in other countries.

TALK IT OVER

DISCUSSION

Discuss this cartoon with your classmates. Then decide what you
think the teacher's response would be.

Shoe by Jeff McNelly

Reprinted by permission: Tribune Media Services.

With help from movies, songs, and TV, many languages have adopted words from other languages. Examples of English words that are used in several languages include *weekend, T-shirt,* and *jogging.* **Franglais? No Way!** discusses the reaction of the French to the introduction of English words in their language.

BEFORE YOU READ

PREREADING ACTIVITY

Make a list of words from English or other languages that have entered your language. Share your list with your classmates.

_____

_____

_____

_____

FIRST READING

Read the article one time quickly for the main ideas.

● ●

Franglais? No Way!

A N N   W O O D B U R Y   M O O R E

1   *M*any American words—thanks to movies, television, pop music, sports, science, and business—have had a dramatic impact on the French language. French students use Americanisms as part of their slang: They wear *un blue-jean*, go *jogging*, and spend *le weekend* listening to *le rock* (music). Adults use American terms to show that they are sophisticated and possess international *know-how*. This Franco-American mixture is called *franglais*, a combination of *français* (French) and *anglais* (English).

2   Many French men and women, however, disapprove of franglais and other foreign influences. They believe that true French, known for its precision and elegance, is being ruined. French was once the international language of diplomacy. Now it ranks eleventh worldwide. Something must be done, they say.

3 In 1975, laws were passed protecting citizens from "language degradation." If equivalent French terms existed, foreign words were banned from government documents, advertising, business contracts, textbooks, and radio and television programs. In addition, all imported goods had to include French instructions.

4 The language laws are enforced by the Commissariat Général de la Langue Française (General Commission of the French Language). The Commissariat upholds its motto, "The French language, it's a pleasure to hear it." It fined a fast-food chain for selling "hamburgers" instead of *steak haché*, and it forced a bottled-water company to drop a pitch for "le fast drink des Alpes." A customs official can even reject an imported shirt labeled "100% acrylic" instead of *100% acrylique*.

5 Terminology Commissions have the immense job of inventing French equivalents—*mots nouveaux* (new words)—for American phrases. The work is time-consuming (more than an hour per word) and tedious (an airliner has more than one million parts—most with English names). Coming up with suitable substitutes is especially difficult in rapidly changing areas of science and technology. When

all else fails, the spelling or pronunciation can be Frenchified. *Manageur* and *pipeline* (pronounced "peep-leen") are examples of the fifteen hundred terms authorized each year.

6   The mots nouveaux have a limited success rate. It is impossible to ban words that people are accustomed to. President Valéry Giscard d'Estaing broke the laws just days after he signed them when he told journalists, "Ce que je vais dire est [what I'm going to tell you is] off the record!" Many new terms are silly: *le baladeur*, for *le Walkman*[1], literally means "the stroller." Others are too long: le cash flow became the tongue-twisting *une marge brute d'autofinancement*.

7   There are many critics of the new program. Some claim that French is too inflexible, too slow to adapt to today's fast-paced, global world. Others find the French approach pompous. After all, many French words are used by Americans (coup d'état, arabesque, déjà vu, élite, avant-garde, détente). U.S. laws may declare English the official language, but forbidding foreign terms is unrealistic. Besides, *all* languages evolve and change. It is a natural process that has gone on for centuries, and no law can stop it.

1Walkman A portable radio-cassette player with headphones.

● ● ● ● ● ● ● ● ● ● ● ● ● ● ● ● ● ● ● ●

IDENTIFYING MAIN IDEAS

The following is a list of main ideas from the article. Locate the paragraphs that contain each idea on the list. Write the number of the paragraph on the line provided.

_____ 1. Many French people disapprove of franglais.

_____ 2. Some people criticize the new French program.

_____ 3. The General Commission of the French Language enforces the language laws.

_____ 4. Many American words are becoming part of the French language.

_____ 5. French equivalents are invented by Terminology Commissions.

_____ 6. Laws passed in 1975 protect the purity of the French language.

_____ 7. The new words are not always successful.

Read the article again more carefully.

Using context from the paragraphs, match the words and phrases on the left with their definitions on the right.

A   **B**

More than a hundred languages are spoken in the school systems of New York City, Chicago, Los Angeles, and Fairfax County, Virginia.

1. mots nouveaux (¶ 5)

2. General Commission of the French Language (¶ 4)

3. coup d'état, déjà vu (¶ 7)

4. Valéry Giscard d'Estaing (¶ 6)

5. franglais (¶ 1)

6. manageur, pipeline (¶ 5)

7. steak haché (¶ 4)

8. "The French language, it's a pleasure to hear it." (¶ 4)

a. law enforcement body

b. hamburger

c. French words used by Americans

d. a combination of French and English words

e. the motto of the General Commission of the French Language

f. English words that have been Frenchified

g. President of France

h. new words

Some people feel that a language is degraded when foreign words enter it. Others feel that languages are organic and that it is natural for them to change. Discuss the ways in which your language has changed over time. In general, do you believe in the purity or in the evolution of language? Give reasons to support your view.

The Benefits of Multilingualism presents interviews with three people whose multilingualism has helped them get ahead. As you read the interviews, note the similarities and differences, which you will be asked about afterward.

The Benefits of Multilingualism

PATRICK ALIAS

Patrick Alias was born and grew up in Lyon, France. He is a businessman who started his career working for an American company that is headquartered in Dusseldorf, Germany. After two years, he changed jobs and went to work for a different American company, this one headquartered in London England. After four years, he was transferred to the company's Tokyo office, where he worked for one year. For the past ten years, he has been working in the United States.

What is your job?

1   I am the Executive Vice President of Sales and Marketing for a high-tech company. I am responsible for sales and marketing, worldwide.

What languages do you speak and how did you learn them?

2   French, of course, which is my native language. German, which I learned in a three-month (eight hours per day) crash course and by living in Germany. English, which I began learning when I was a child. I was ten years old when I first went to live with a family in England. Italian, which I learned for business purposes when I was working in Europe. And Japanese, which I am learning now. I have a tutor whom I work with here, and I go to Japan almost every other month on business.

In what ways have these languages helped your career?

3   They have made my career! I couldn't have done what I've done without languages. When I worked for an American company in Germany, I was very useful because I could communicate in the biggest European markets— France, England, and Germany. But, specifically in terms of sales and marketing, languages are one of the keys to my success. Learning the language helps me to understand the people of a country better, and therefore, I do a better job. People don't buy from me because they like me; they buy from me because they think I understand them. Language is just an expression of a culture. When I used to go to Sweden and Denmark, I always looked at their languages, although we communicated in English. I looked at their languages so I could see how the people think. I think that the sounds of a language reflect the artistic aspects of the people and the grammar reflects their organization.

4   You know, even when I was a young boy, aged ten or so, I never understood why we had borders and passports and baggage checks. I didn't see why every country had to be different. I wanted to be in contact with the world. Now, of course, everything is changing.

ALISON HOWE

Alison Howe grew up in Rochester, New York. She has always loved languages and has learned more of them than many of us ever will. She has lived and worked overseas for over fifteen years—in four countries and in Hawaii.

What is your job?

5   I work at the Harvard Institute for International Development. I am the Project Administrator for the Central and Eastern European Environmental Economic Policy Project. In this job, I do not use my languages on a day-to-day basis, but I am working in an international context and my languages come in handy. Most of my work is dedicated to managing the needs of the consultants in the ten central and eastern European countries we work with.

What languages do you speak and how did you learn them?

6   I began learning French in kindergarten and continued until my first year in college. I took Latin in high school. I learned Dutch when I lived with a host family in the Netherlands for a year. I was seventeen years old at the time and this was when I discovered that I was good at picking up languages. My Dutch friends said that I had a "Taal-Knobel," a special language bump on my head! I knew then that I wanted to pursue my interest in languages and cultures. In college, I majored in German and spent my third year studying in Vienna. I began to study Japanese when I was at the University of Hawaii and then continued while I was living in Japan for three years. It sounds crazy, but I learned to speak Spanish in Sweden—from Latin American students. And of course, I also learned Swedish in Sweden. I lived there for seven years while working at a university that was associated with the United Nations.

In what ways have these languages helped your career?

7   Let me point out that though I have "learned" many languages, I have not mastered them in the same way that a professional interpreter or translator has. Still, they have opened doors for me. They have made me seek jobs in international contexts and helped me get those jobs. Like many people who have studied or lived overseas for awhile, I got bitten by the bug. I can't imagine living my professional or social life without international interactions or what you might call a multicultural backdrop. I have found that I cannot be happy unless I have access to intercultural contacts. Since 1977, I have spent much more time abroad than in the United States. I like going to new places, eating new foods, and experiencing new cultures. If you can speak the language, it's easier to get to know the country and its people. If I had the time and money, I would live for a year in as many countries as possible.

8   Beyond my career, my facility with languages has given me a few rare opportunities. Once, just after I returned from my year in Vienna, I was asked to translate for a German judge at an Olympic-level horse event. I learned a lot about the sport. In Japan, once when I was in the studio audience of a TV cooking show, I was asked to go up on the stage and taste the beef dish that was being prepared and give my reactions. They asked "Was it as good as American beef?" It was very exciting for me to be on Japanese TV speaking in Japanese about how delicious the beef was.

THIDARAT SIRIPHATIVIRAT

Thidarat Siriphativirat was born in Bangkok, Thailand. Her father is a businessman who does a lot of traveling. Like her father, Thidarat has always wanted a career that involves travel, and with a degree in international business law, she will be able to do just that. When she finished her law degree in Thailand, Thidarat worked in a multinational law firm. She recently received a scholarship to study in the United States.

What is your job?

9   The law firm where I worked in Thailand specialized in intellectual properties, such as trademarks, patents, and copyrights; and communications, including computer systems, video, and satellite.

10   My clients come from all over the world. I do legal research and give advice to my clients. Sometimes, I represent them in court.

What languages do you know and how did you learn them?

11   My native language is Thai, but in my house we spoke both Thai and Cantonese. My Chinese grandmother lived with us, so I grew up bilingual. I learned German in an intensive language program and I have studied English since high school.

In what ways have these languages helped you in your career?

12   Working in a multinational law firm, I have to deal with clients from many different countries. Knowing how to communicate with them in their native language is very advantageous. I am much more successful when I know the native language. I am able to expand my client base and handle their legal matters more efficiently. I also have to travel to other countries when my clients need me. Sometimes I have to attend meetings and present my research in English.

HOW WELL DID YOU READ?

The three people interviewed share some of the same goals and skills but come from varied backgrounds. Read the following list and write the initial of the person (or people) that each item applies to: *P* for Patrick, *A* for Alison, and *T* for Thidarat. If the statement does not apply to any of the people interviewed, leave it blank.

1. _____ grew up bilingual.

2. _____ speaks Spanish.

3. _____ lived abroad.

4. _____ emigrated from a foreign country.

5. _____ studied a foreign language in college.

6. _____ taught abroad.

7. _____ speaks Cantonese.

8. _____ wants to find a new job.

9. _____ lived with a family in another country.

10. _____ is interested in other cultures.

11. _____ speaks Japanese.

12. _____ has had a job in a foreign country.

13. _____ learned German in an intensive language course.

14. _____ is a professional translator.

FYi

Since 1901, 30 percent of the U.S. Nobel prize-winners have been immigrants to the United States.

TALK IT OVER

DISCUSSION

It is clear from the interviews that these three people are successful in their chosen careers. Based on the information in the interviews, discuss the characteristics that they have in common.

1. In pairs, discuss how learning English or another second language fits in with your educational and career goals. Interview each other and take notes. Be sure to include the following information:

   a. Reasons for studying a second language
   b. How knowledge of another language will be useful in terms of career, travel, or education

2. Then write a profile for your partner, using the style and format of the interviews you read. Choose at least one quotation from your interview that you would use as a caption for a picture of your partner.

3. Compare your results with those of your classmates. Does the profile of you accurately describe your aspirations?

This quotation is taken from an article entitled "The Global Village Finally Arrives." After you read it, answer the questions that follow.

This is a typical day of a relatively typical soul in today's diversified world. I wake up to the sound of my Japanese clock radio, put on a T-shirt sent to me by an uncle in Nigeria and walk out into the street, past German cars, to my office. Around me are English-language students from Korea, Switzerland and Argentina—all on this Spanish-named road in this Mediterranean-style town. On TV, I find the news is in Mandarin; today's baseball game is being broadcast in Korean. For lunch I can walk to a sushi-bar, a tandoori palace, a Thai cafe, or the latest burrito joint (run by an old Japanese lady). Who am I, I sometimes wonder, the son of Indian parents and a British citizen who spends much of his time in Japan (and is therefore—what else?—an American permanent resident)? And where am I?

I am, as it happens, in Southern California, in a quiet, relatively uninternational town, but I could easily be in Vancouver or Sydney or London or Hong Kong. All the world's a rainbow coalition, more and more; the whole world, you might say, is going global.[1]

1Pico Iyer, *Time Special Issue* (Fall 1993), 86.

COMPREHENSION CHECK

1. Make a list of the international references the author makes.

_____

_____

_____

2. What do you think Iyer means by "All the world's a rainbow coalition . . . "? Why does he use the word _rainbow_?

_____

_____

_____

There are approximately 6,000 languages spoken in the world today. Of these languages, 845 are spoken in one country: India. The language spoken by the largest number of people is Mandarin Chinese. It is spoken by more than 800 million people.

3. Iyer mentions several kinds of ethnic restaurants that are in his neighborhood. What kinds of international restaurants are there in your neighborhood?

_____

_____

_____

4. He also says that several TV programs are broadcast in foreign languages. Is that true in your country? If so, what kinds of shows are broadcast in other languages?

_____

_____

_____

5. Iyer is wearing a T-shirt from Nigeria. How international are the clothes you are wearing?

_____

_____

_____

209

JUST FOR FUN

ANAGRAM

A	L	B	
T	I	L	O
A	I	Z	
O	G	N	

Make as many words as you can using the letters in the boxes. However, in this anagram, the letter "o" must occur in every word you make. Proper nouns and non-English words are not allowed. Write your words in the spaces below.

1. _____

2. _____

3. _____

4. _____

5. _____

6. _____

7. _____

8. _____

9. _____

10. _____

POSTREADING DISCUSSION QUESTIONS

1. Many people worry that globalization will result in the loss of culture and the cultural identity of individual countries. How do you feel about this? Do you believe that a loss of cultural identity may occur? If so, do you feel that would be bad?

2. In an article describing travel on earth in the future, Isaac Asimov said, "Increasingly there will be travel on earth only for people who want to see old friends and relatives and actually touch them, or who want to

see the sites of the world. It will be easy for them to do this, for the people who would be crowding around with them on business will be doing that business at home."[1] Is it realistic to think that as communication improves, travel for business will become unnecessary? What would this mean in terms of foreign language study?

3. Stephen Wolf is the Chairman and Chief Executive Officer of United Airlines. In an article called "The Olympic Spirit" he said, "Certainly, if 80 nations can come together in the name of sport, the possibility exists for breaking down barriers to more significant ends. Indeed, [many] opportunities for global cooperation exist—from securing peace in war-torn nations to preserving the environment across national lines to opening channels of free trade around the world."[2] In your own words, express what you think Mr. Wolf is saying.

4. Language and business are not the only areas in which globalization is occurring. Look at the following list and discuss the impact of globalization on each.

a. education
b. medicine
c. law
d. the arts
e. food

f. the environment
g. communication
h. sports
i. trade
j. technology

What other areas can be added to this list?

_____

_____

_____

_____

_____

READER'S JOURNAL

Before you write your last Reader's Journal, take some time to think about the many issues that globalization involves. As a foreign language student, you are a part of the process of globalization. Write for ten to twenty minutes on any topic relating to globalization.

1Isaac Asimov, "Futureworld: Travel on Earth," *Boy's Life* (October 1990), 61.
2*Hemispheres* (March 1994), 13.

READER'S JOURNAL

Date: _____

_____

_____

_____

_____

_____

_____

_____

_____

_____

_____

_____

_____

_____

_____

_____

_____

_____

_____

_____

_____

_____

UNIT 1   **JUST FOR FUN**   page 26

WORD SCRAMBLE

1. kiss, 2. gestures, 3. broom, 4. tourist, 5. sniff, 6. journal, 7. custom, 8. signature, 9. information

UNIT 2   **JUST FOR FUN**   page 58

WORD SEARCH

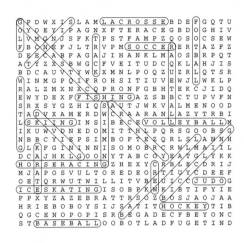

UNIT 3   **JUST FOR FUN**   page 88

SCRAMBLE

1. lines, 2. Thor, 3. NASA, 4. ice, 5. galaxy, 6. theories, 7. messages, 8. South Seas, 9. earthlings, 10. mysteries

UNIT 5   **JUST FOR FUN**   page 142

CROSSWORD PUZZLE

Across: 1. consumer, 2. profit, 3. scam, 4. seller, 5. stress, 6. outrage, 7. jeans, 8. rivets, 9. bargain, 10. fraud, 11. logo, 12. catalogue, 13. savvy, 14. smell, 15. brand, 16. flooded

Down: 1. compensation, 2. norm, 3. strut, 4. spender, 5. odor, 6. gender, 7. strategy, 8. patent, 9. sniff, 10. audience, 11. negotiate, 12. tricky, 13. slogan, 14. switch, 15. label, 16. draw

UNIT 6   **JUST FOR FUN**   page 166

PALINDROMES, OXYMORONS, PLEONASMS

1. ple, 2. pal, 3. oxy, 4. pal, 5. pal, 6. oxy, 7. ple, 8. pal, 9. pal, 10. oxy, 11. pal, 12. oxy, 13. pal, 14. oxy, 15. oxy, 16. oxy, 17. oxy, 18. pal, 19. oxy, 20. oxy, 21. ple, 22. oxy, 23. oxy, 24. pal, 25. oxy, 26. oxy

HOMONYMS

1. sea/see, 2. flee/flea, 3. red/read, 4. toe/tow, 5. blue/blew, 6. threw/through, 7. weight/wait

UNIT 7   **JUST FOR FUN**   page 190

WORD GAME

1. an umbrella, 2. avoid ladders, 3. step on cracks, 4. spill salt, 5. thirteen, 6. nests, 7. a shooting star, 8. rabbit's foot, 9. Tutankhamen's tomb, 10. breaking a mirror

Greenland Sea

Norwegian Sea

SWEDEN

CZECHOSLOVAKIA

FINLAND

THE
ETHERLANDS

NORWAY

R U S S I A

North Sea

IRELAND

ENGLAND

GERMANY

A S I A

BELGIUM

EUROPE

BULGARIA

FRANCE

YUGOSLOVIA

ITALY

Black Sea

SPAIN

GREECE

MALTA

*Sea of
Japan*

TUNISIA

Mediterranean Sea

C H I N A

JAPAN

ALGERIA

EGYPT

INDIA

Arabian Sea

TAIWAN

AFRICA

*Bay of
Bengal*

THAILAND

*South China
Sea*

Philippine Sea

NIGERIA

MALAYSIA

Indian Ocean

Java Sea

AUSTRALIA

SOUTH
AFRICA

*South
Atlantic
Ocean*

215